TRUTH, WAR, AND THE DREAM-GAME

LAWRENCE FIXEL

TRUTH, WAR, AND THE DREAM-GAME

Selected Prose Poems and Parables, 1966-1990

COFFEE HOUSE PRESS :: MINNEAPOLIS :: 1991

The following appeared in *The Scale of Silence* (Kayak, 1970), a previous collection of parables: "The Crossing," "The Choice," "The Master," "The Invaders." "The Master" also appeared in *Imperial Messages: One Hundred Modern Parables, An International Anthology* edited by Howard Schwartz (Avon, 1976). "The Shrinking City" appeared in *Unscheduled Departures, The Asylum Anthology of Short Fiction* edited by Greg Boyd (1991). "The Life and Death of a Guide" appeared first as a Mencard on the occasion of my seventieth birthday, January 7, 1987 (Menard Press, London, Anthony Rudolf, editor). It was published again in *Caliban* 2, 1987 (Ann Arbor, Lawrence R. Smith, editor). Others of these pieces have been published in *Alcatraz, Bottomfish, City Lights Review, New American Writing, The Expatriate Review, Madrona, G. P. W. I. T. D., Poetry Flash, Notus* and *Talisman*.

Special thanks to Jo-Anne Rosen and Ruhama Veltfort for their dedication and skill in making this work accessible to the publisher, and to all those at Coffee House Press for their effort in converting a manuscript of diverse intentions into a coherent book. Thanks one more time to Stephanie Sanchez for the cover and accompanying illustrations, and to Mark Citret for his photograph.

The publisher thanks the following for their support of this project: The Bush Foundation; First Bank System Foundation; Minnesota State Arts Board; the National Endowment for the Arts, a federal agency; and Northwest Area Foundation.

Coffee House Press books are available to bookstores through our primary distributor, Consortium Book Sales and Distribution, 287 East Sixth Street, Suite 365, St Paul, Minnesota 55101. Our books are also available through all major library distributors and jobbers, and through most small press distributors, including Bookpeople, Bookslinger, Inland, Pacific Pipeline, and Small Press Distribution. For personal orders, catalogs, or other information, write to: Coffee House Press, 27 North Fourth Street, Minneapolis, MN 55401.

Library of Congress Cataloging-in-publication data

Fixel, Lawrence

    Truth, war, and the dream-game / selected prose poems and parables, 1966-1990 / Lawrence Fixel

       p.   cm.

    ISBN 0-918273-88-9 : $10.95

    1. Prose poems, American. 2. Parables. I. Title

PS3556.I96T78 1992   91-35572

811'.54—dc20   CIP

Arrangements such as the layout of a city or building, a set of
tools, a display of merchandise, the verbal exposition of facts or
ideas . . . are called orderly when an observer or listener can grasp
their overall structure."

—Rudolf Arnheim

"Meaning then is an indication of something beyond mere
existence, either an end and aim, or the notion of form . . . . Any
action, design, quest, or search carries meaning as purpose, any
work of art is meaning as form."

—Erich Kahler

"All these parables really set out to say merely that the
incomprehensible is incomprehensible, and we know that already.
But the cares we have to struggle with every day: that is a
different matter."

—Franz Kafka

for Justine: this time with time as measure

Contents

Chance Scripts

Structural Pursuits

Foreword

Written over a long period of time, the three texts included here—*Tracking Stations, Chance Scripts, Structural Pursuits*—involve both retrospect and prospect. That is, they are part of a still evolving effort. The primary text, *Tracking Stations*, completed in 1981, was offered for publication by itself. I have left it here unchanged as an example of "making a case" for what a specific genre, the parable, has to offer.

I realized then that the ancient parable, as a brief narrative, sometimes with an explicit moral, sometimes as riddle or enigma, still provoked controversy: in the conflicting interpretations of readers, critics, scholars. But in contrast to a living form, it might be considered vestigial, an anachronism. The modern parable, still not widely known, was assigned largely to the seminal examples of Kafka and Borges and their penetrating, often devastating illumination of a world split between psyche, spirit, and material concerns. At present, however, an increasing number of writers are finding in the parable a flexible, versatile instrument especially suited to convey the distilled essences of a fragmented world.

For my own part, I felt the challenge of finding other realms for subject and theme: for instance, the more neglected immediate issues of politics and war, religious cults, terrorism, etc. At the same time, I felt the need to articulate a particular view. I found this in the observation that both the ancient and modern parable often involved the overthrow of an expectation: the reversal of some deep-grounded assumption or explicit belief. Examples of this could be found not only in Kafka and Borges, but in Jesus, Kierkegaard, and Brecht. Even further, the continuum could be extended to Heraclitus, to the Midrash, to the Zen koan, the Sufi story. Over this whole panorama, paradox is a key element, opposing the identity of opposites to any commonsense, linear, or literal view. Specifically, I found a particular use of metaphor as analog: juxtaposing actual, virtual, and fictional worlds, transposing and connecting the different scales, planes, and dimensions of reality.

At this point it may be useful to offer some minimum distinction between prose poem and parable. As I see it, the parable is required to be *about something*—something which connects with, even though it conflicts with, our sense of the world. Thus it challenges our assumptions while, paradoxically, it evokes some feeling of universality. The prose poem, characteristically, as its name implies, is viewed from its ambiguous location, somewhere between poetry and prose. Thus it tends to be lyrical, subjective, impressionistic. Based more on self-expression than the combination of concept and metaphor offered by the parable, it can provide a counterpoint of *possibility* to balance the parable's greater concern with *necessity*.

There is more to be said about the passage from *Tracking Stations* to *Truth, War, and the Dream-Game*. In brief, I continued writing, exploring, until the boundaries between "prose poem" and "parable" shifted and narrowed. Again, in retrospect, this appears mainly as a shift in emphasis from "content" to "form." Specifically, it involved more latitude for a free play of the mind: for impulse to have an equal share with intention. This, I suggest, is indicated by the very titles of the more recent work: *Chance Scripts* and *Structural Pursuits.* It is hoped that, while each piece is a discrete entity, the reader can envision further: behind this a shared, perceivable world.

There are some other considerations which I have left for the "Afterword." These concern the possibility of readings and rereadings based more on thematic content. The last point here is that words on a page need to be released and renewed in the reader's mind. Released to acquire—whatever thought or feeling they may evoke—their own subsequent history. So that a work of words may join the play of mind—join in a kind of dance, where meanings remain to be dreamed upon, not finally determined.

Lawrence Fixel, March 1991

Tracking Stations
New and Selected Parables
1966–1981

Part One: The Flight / The Quest

"We live in a time when flight and quest bear the closest resemblance."

"No longer objects of compassion, they seem to have reached— and settled into—some realm we are not permitted to enter."

Flight Patterns

"Between the void and the sheer event..."
—Valéry

1.

It is said, of the millions who undertake the journey, that the greatest number are lost somewhere along the way. To prove this, evidence is produced, statistics gathered, witnesses summoned. There are even films of the long, straggling procession, which presumably reveal the fate of the missing. Yet it appears no one—ourselves included—is deterred by this, for it is equally intolerable to remain where we are.

2.

. . . Word continues to arrive from monitors at the highly equipped tracking stations. They report a whole series of unexplained dots and dashes on the flickering screens. Even the most experienced observers—using the most advanced techniques—concede that the habitual flight patterns can no longer be interpreted. . . .

3.

I have seen some of the incoming messages. They bear such strange notations as "missing in action," "dead on arrival," etc. With so many different languages, from such different worlds, the gap between what is transmitted and received continues to widen.

4.

I have resolved not to be upset by any of this. To limit myself to what can be verified by sensory evidence. One thing is clear: whether we travel the direct route of desire, or detours of illusion, we still miss connection. Something is *there*—ahead of or behind us—and we are drawn in that direction. For a time we seem to have arrived . . . . But as the wind changes, the mist descends, we can no longer tell where we are.

5.

Let us suppose, for instance, that you have been where I have been. We meet one afternoon in a village in a neighboring country.... Joining the crowd in the plaza, we observe the stately walk of the costumed women. Moving on, we notice in contrast the immobility of the vendors: the heavy bodies squatting beside the earthen jars.

6.

Is the scene familiar? Then let memory take a further step: to that moment when armed men in gray uniforms appear.... Suddenly we feel a sharp intersection of competing gestures, of inviting and disturbing fragrances. Someone drops petals in front of the candle-lit altar; someone else throws poisoned meat to the hungry dogs.... Speaking of this later, disturbed by our fragmented impressions, the question arises: What name can we give to this land?

7.

We may of course continue the search, each producing letters, photographs, documents. Or simply recognize that, between any two witnesses, we can expect these differences. Each might then retreat into a private retrospect.... But what if we decide to give up these wanderings, returning to this body, this present time? It may then occur to us that what signifies this world is nothing else but the current of our feeling. And as for the flesh that dissolves, disappears, who can say it will not appear again? If not in this form, this familiar image, then perhaps as an *intention* that moves through silence and the quickening wind.

1978/1979

Above It All

"Destiny, if you thought I had the potential for departure, you should have given me wings."
                                                            —Pierre Reverdy

If God intended us to fly . . . . The proverb becomes a cliché, a joke, then disappears. But not entirely. With our desire to ascend, to sail through the air, comes also a sense of transgression. We go so far, so fast, carried along by sheer momentum. Then suddenly something happens to remind us that—unlike cloud, bird or star —here we are intruders.

*

Remember the tale of "The Horse with One Wing"? For those who don't, it goes like this: Once there was a band of wild horses who roamed freely in open space. Then came settlers who captured and tamed them. Still later came those whose secret intention was to turn them into food for domestic pets. . . . One day, as the story goes, one of the horses noticed a small wing growing out of his side. He would run with the others, then find a place alone. There he began leaping, dreaming of flight. When the band was reduced to a few survivors, he knew it was time. He ran to the edge of a nearby cliff . . . .

*

Intolerable alternatives—are there no others? It would seem that there are those who still persist in their search. Even now someone is at work in a garage, a small shed, to find a solution. Not far from where we live, there is one almost ready. Some morning soon, a figure will appear on a roof, waiting to lift off. Not an apparition, I assure you, but someone like ourselves . . . .

*

I write this as testimony, this fifteenth day of April, 1980. The same calendar tells me also: *born this day in 1452, Leonardo da Vinci.*

7

Give Up, Give Up

As Kafka tells it: a man wandering in a strange city notices a policeman standing nearby. He hesitates, then decides to approach and ask directions . . . . Stopping here, we might expect a familiar response, appropriate to the ordinary situation. This is quickly shattered, however, by the extraordinary reply: "Give up. Give up."

In the absence of further details in the original, I have invented some that would soften the impact, make the reply sound less absolute. I have even written a story that—however intended at the time—now appears as a kind of response . . .

*

. . . *Stephen X.* has escaped from a prisoner of war camp. He wanders through a procession of deserting soldiers, refugees in a nation falling apart, close to revolution. . . . When the policeman approaches, he has to choose whether to remain or to run. Deciding to stay, his mind forms a desperate strategy: "To reach the man beneath the uniform, I would speak of his own family, loved ones, their need for peace and survival." In my story then, the appeal is successful: the policeman responds, directing him to a place where he finds food and shelter.

*

If the reference to the "fiction" is not enough, I offer something from my own experience. It was many years ago; I was then perhaps twenty or twenty-one, hitchhiking through the southern part of this country. It was my very first journey; I still pictured myself as an unarmed "wanderer" in a hostile world . . . . When the man in uniform came toward me, I remembered stories of vagrants being jailed, sentenced to hard labor. So that when he spoke, I could hardly hear what he was saying. When I was able to sort it out, I finally realized the kind intention . . . .

*

Kindness or cruelty—so far I have looked at it only from one side. The picture changes when I also recognize in *myself* the one who wears the uniform. And in this role I have to ask, have to remember: what has been my response? For reasons I cannot now pretend to understand, I have at times turned away with indifference and cruelty.

So that there remains—as in a disturbing, recurring dream—the image of one who continues to wear the disordered clothes of the wanderer. The one who must wait, without protection and without certainty, for the figure coming toward him: *so do ye unto me.*

1979

9

Destruction of the Temple

"Finally, because of its situation at the center of the cosmos,
the temple or the sacred city is always the meeting point of the three
cosmic regions: heaven, earth, hell."

—Mircea Eliade

1.

First the incident on the airstrip, then the even more shocking news: the "slaughter" of nearly a thousand men, women, and children. What is still not certain, as I write this, is whether murder or suicide is involved. Like everyone else, I wonder how it started, why it ended this way. But even to begin to understand, one would need to know who these people were, what they were searching for. Also it seems, something to help explain the extraordinary power and magnetism of their leader.

2.

As the days go by, there is talk about *The Temple* as an unfortunate attempt by those without power and influence to create a community outside the laws that bind us together. Inevitably the words *utopia* and *paradise* are heard, sounding strange in this secular, cynical time. I am reminded of certain dark events, centuries ago, when groups of *heretics* went to their deaths. Am I wrong in recalling that, through periods of persecution and torture, the victims experienced a kind of *ecstasy*?

3.

. . . All this passes through my mind, as I read the letters of Q. and N., which arrived today. They write from different parts of the world, offering sympathy along with their views on what has happened. What remains in my mind are their notions that *The Temple*, like any other structure, is subject to decay and dissolution. For any form to contain a substance, it must be flexible enough to withstand the pull of conflicting desires. At other times I might be grateful for the metaphysical speculation, the extravagant mind-play. This time, however, I feel their elegant reasoning as an intrusion—as if upon a simple private grief of my own....

4.

...I have started daily walks in the neighborhood, feeling it better to be outside—away from the enclosed space of walls and mirrors. Occasionally I stop in where coffee and wine are served, taking the opportunity for brief, casual conversation. While the subject is not mentioned directly, it is clear the fate of *The Temple* is on everyone's mind....

5.

I still do not feel ready to respond to Q. and N. But I am spending more time at home, doing the usual chores, reading and writing in my notebook. Yesterday I made the following entry: *Each time we search for light, a greater darkness enters.* I started to cross this out, then decided to leave it in; later I added: *What can we do without the visible Heaven, the tangible Hell?*

6.

The bodies have arrived in metal coffins. We're told that, after a while, those that can be identified will be shipped to their *city of origin.* (Curious that the word *home* is not used in these accounts.) Besides the walks, I have been taking buses and streetcars to unfamiliar sections of the city. And writing in my notebook: *The world wavers in my sight. It grows harder to tell who or what we are.*

7.

Some days ago I finally wrote—just brief notes—to Q. and N. I merely thanked them for their letters, said I was well, promised to write again when I had time and energy. Even this much was a great effort, since I felt absent, encased in silence. I have made no plans, beyond routine things that have to be done, for today, tomorrow or the following days. I will continue writing here—not with hope of understanding or release—but only as long as I recognize my own voice....

1978—revised 1979

The Departure / The Return

Zero, as he has chosen to be called, signals his comrades and moves up the steps to enter the plane. He is a robust man, tall and with a thick black moustache. At the moment, with success of the operation almost assured, his whole being expresses exultation . . . . This takes place after he and a dozen followers—using numbers instead of names—enter the government palace and, with perfect timing, emerge with the "emblems" of power. The quality and rank of the hostages—an Archbishop, a General, two Ambassadors—indicates what they have achieved . . . In a short while the plane takes off. Nervous moments follow as government planes appear; but as these veer off, without further pursuit, confidence and exhilaration return. The flight continues without incident; less than an hour later—securing asylum in a neighboring country—they make a safe landing.

*

At the palace, the besieged Dictator is being interviewed. Facing the "eyes and ears of the world," he declares it is better to suffer this momentary humiliation than the loss of so many lives. (Whether he actually says "innocent" lives is not clear from the translation.) He also lets it be known that, in making this decision, he has been guided by the traditional values of Family and Religion. (Curiously, his voice and manner express the same sense of exultation shown by his opponent.)

*

As the news broadcast shifts to another subject, the Poet presses a button that blanks the screen. All this, he tells himself, has happened over and over again. The names and titles of the rulers change, but for the *ruled*, the round of days remains the same . . . . Some time later, still unable to return to more immediate concerns, he drifts into reverie . . . . What emerges is a figure on a platform facing a huge crowd. On the very streets now being besieged, there stands the indigenous Poet—(Brother? Comrade?)—returned from long exile . . . . Something must have happened *there and then* which cannot be forgotten. Suddenly he experiences, as if in a real present, in his own flesh, the expectancy of the crowd. He stands beside them as Rubén Darío begins reciting "The Motives of the Wolf."

1979/1981

The Refugees / The Pilgrims

1.

Seated at the table, we look for what we remember: the gentle enthusiast, at home on his own small plot of ground. Also for the changes, in the intervening years, since he started working with the dispossessed. We notice then that his speech is softer, slower, that his hands more often gesture uncertainty. We try to imagine that part of his life: visiting refugee camps, disaster areas, talking to officials unable, unwilling to listen . . . .

2.

This is T.'s report: You see the ordinary life—which at one moment seems unalterable—thrown into turmoil, beyond intention and control. For instance, on a given day, a small boat leaves the mainland. It is poorly equipped, with an inexperienced crew. On board are dozens, even hundreds, with just the few belongings they can carry. We call them "refugees"—not exiles or outcasts—to indicate the lack of choice . . . . On another day we receive word: a plane has crashed; there are so many victims, so many survivors. In this case, the passengers were "pilgrims" on their way from another continent to visit the sacred shrines . . . .

3.

He goes on: Between the plane that crashes and the boat sunk by gunfire or swamped by the tides, there is some connection. But what is it? We think of refugees as homeless, dispossessed. And pilgrims as on a journey, on their way somewhere, devoted and highly motivated. Yet they both seem dislocated, and in some sense interchangeable . . . .

4.

Why is T. telling us this? Is there something he wants to reconcile in himself, a feeling of being dispersed, becoming part of the endless stream of the wanderers, the uprooted? Before this, we

14

recall, he told us anecdotes, stories that illustrated problems related to solutions. This time, however, the tone is uneasy, the voice of an inward questioning....

5.

With dinner finished, we sit facing the lights of the familiar city. T. looks at his watch, mentions the hour of the departing plane. We are used to these short visits, knowing that he goes when he has to, wherever he is summoned .... Time for one more account, though, of that part of the world where everything, a whole nation, can be overturned: "They closed the borders, sealed the cities. Yet one group who got away—not believing what they were told—demanded to be sent back. We helped them, since this is what they wanted. They went back across— about fifty of them—and vanished...."

6.

Twilight around us; the sky thick with clouds. T. seems already on his way, gone somewhere beyond us .... I wonder now what T. has failed to tell us. *The refugees. The pilgrims.* His example of those who travel by boat, by plane, leaves something out .... I think of the solitary figures, walking across the dry land. I see them bent and bony, leaning on a stick—going nowhere. Visible only to the barking dogs, in the most remote villages. What can we say about these—immemorial wanderers—for whom we have no name?

7.

We say goodbye, watch him turn and wave before entering the waiting taxi. We close the door, return to the table as night comes on. It has not yet come through to us—(the thought arrives later, just before sleep)—that we live in a time when flight and quest bear the closest resemblance.

1978

15

The Base Camp

I have seen their attention wander, their eyes looking toward the door, when the survivors speak. And it would be foolish, a waste of time, to try to change this. What I write here then is for myself, for those who care to remember . . . . There is no flag, no plaque, nothing left to mark the place. Yet it is *there*, as real, as tangible as the mountain itself. For without that what would I be—what would *we* have been?

I have been told it is best to remain silent. To let the others, those who come after, have their say. Well then, listen to their voices: *Whatever it was, it is gone. With our new strength, improved equipment, we have moved the Base Camp farther than they ever dreamed possible . . . .* I recognize the tone, the self-assured authority. But then I remember: The tents lashed against the wind, the sky blurred and gray, the unknown towering over us . . . . How closely we worked together, moved together, as if gathered under a single name. How vivid those moments, whether climbing or staying behind . . . *Staying behind:* when and how did that become a choice? What was it like then, waving goodbye to the few who insisted on that final, vertical assault—and were never seen again?

*

. . . Feeling anchored, at peace, in this warm, familiar room. Sifting through those lost days and hours, there is nothing I can retrieve or rearrange. Whatever has to be confronted, now or later, will not change the outcome. Surely it is enough to have shared those hazards, gone that far. I need not recognize the one who never wanted to leave, to step outside the safety of this room.

1981

Absent Without Leave

They have not, as of this writing, been in attendance. And from all indications, they do not plan to attend. This in spite of the various inducements, prizes still being offered. On rare occasions, however, one stands before us: the dark face impenetrable, the words openly or implicitly accusing. . . . And after the departure, what are we left with? The sense of yet another world, closing in on itself, shut off from sight. Inevitably, we are reminded of our own presences and absences, of the distance between desire and fulfillment. Yet how to compare this with their struggle to achieve *visibility?*

*

All this, I realize now, is somewhat misleading. It does not take into account how incredibly much the world has changed. For as it now appears, it is the *invisible* who are less vulnerable, less easily targeted. No longer objects of compassion, they seem to have reached—and settled into—some realm we are not permitted to enter. And where we still wait to be invited . . . . But the invitation does not arrive. And when we open our passports, stare at the photos, we suddenly notice: *Not valid for travel in* . . . . We remember something peculiar about the signs at the various terminals. There was always one that pointed toward "access"; while another, just beside it, seemed to indicate "refuge." With this in mind, we begin to wonder whether there is a travel agent —one with more knowledge, more influence—who could arrange . . .

1981

17

The Crossing

1.

It is twilight when we reach the border. (Late summer: our first crossing.) The long line of cars. The slow inching forward. Ahead, dark-faced men in creased uniforms. Stepping out of the glass-enclosed booths, they reach for and examine the folded papers, then gesture this way, that way. We cannot tell what it means, but it seems that some will go through at once while others have further questions to answer. We take it for granted that we will be among the latter....

And so it turns out. We are directed to a low building off to the side. There we enter a small, square room: plain wooden benches, watermarked walls, the faces of those who wait to learn which way they are going.

Asking the questions, the bored official scratches his neck, waves at the flies that circle the document in his hand. Finally he nods, goes to the typewriter. Placing the forms before us, he indicates where to sign. Holding the pen, our hands are wet; our fingers tremble.

But we are not through yet. Outside, another one goes through our boxes and suitcases. (Is there something whose presence we cannot explain?) He walks away. We wait, still unaware of what has been decided. The man returns, places a small disk on the windshield. And as we remain motionless, he shrugs, points toward the road that lies ahead.

2.

We are disobeying the injunction not to travel at night. Of course it has all been explained: the condition of the road, what has happened to other travelers, etc. Thus we are reminded the journey is our own choice, our own responsibility.

All of this comes to mind as the light slowly disappears. What matters now is this narrow strip of black asphalt; our purpose and presence centered on the turning blades, the revolving wheels. We soon notice and are disturbed by the absence of the white line. And there is no space beside the road if we should have to stop. In the swelling darkness, we sense the solid pavement falling away—a weightless descent into nothingness.

. . . Lights in the distance. After what seems like a long interval, they remain the same size and in the same position. At last the lights of cars coming toward us. (Will there be some notice, sign of recognition?) Nothing happens. The space widens, darkens as they go past. And it appears as though we are going toward what they are in flight from.

. . . Remembering the warning, we watch for the appearance of animals. And from time to time, they materialize: white shapes with burning underwater eyes. We are not prepared, though, for the walkers: tattered clothing, bare legs, some kind of weight on their backs. They straighten and stiffen under the headlights.

3.

The air thickens. A long time since we have exchanged a word. Yellow knives slash the fabric of night. All the signs of impending storm—yet here we cannot tell. The dry tongue searches the dry mouth. Clothing sticks to the skin . . . . Now we are in it, but there is no name or precedent. (Knives and drums warring in the sky— but no downpour follows.) It is as though, having strayed into some off-limits area, we are being tested, forced to validate our presence. (Borders within and borders beyond.) But not knowing the purpose, what is expected, one can only hold tight to the wheel, continue staring through the windshield . . . .

4.

All this is behind us; we have indeed passed through the interminable night. Whatever it was that threatened, whatever related the shapes outside and those in our minds, the "attack" went no further than this. (The swarm of insects, the gray bird that splashed against the windshield.) Perhaps then this is the nature of the test: to withstand the assault on our senses, to contain and integrate what is there and what we are forced to imagine.

. . . Crossing the dry river bed, seeing the first volcano, the first convoluted growth of jungle. With night turning into day, we found ourselves involved in some vast metamorphosis, with that whole panorama—animals, plants, the earth itself—moving into light. What does it mean: this sense of passage from one state of being to another?

5.

Entering the town, we make inquiries. After a few wrong turns, we locate the narrow, tree-lined street. We drive carefully across the brown cobblestones—trying also to limit our anticipation—and at last come to the house.

A servant answers the bell. We are led to the back of the house, and then into the garden. A few minutes later the woman—whom we have not seen for years—appears. She stands there for a moment, among the flowers, the fruit trees, the bright-colored birds. Then with a smile, her arms extended, she comes toward us.

6.

In spite of the welcome, the warm exchange, it soon becomes clear that we live in different worlds. We have passed through the long night and emerged, but still our identity depends on where we have come from. But she has made another commitment: to these orange flowers, these green and yellow birds. And to these dark-faced people. She seems ready to share not only their songs, but their diseases. (Waking to find rats streaming across the floor. Being operated upon by the local doctor—the surgery performed on a plain wooden table.)

And so we leave the following day. For her the encounter could be no more than an interlude. For she has crossed over—to the other side of things. She may at times look back—but only to see how far she has come. Our presence, any protection we might offer, is no longer relevant.

7.

We go further into the dry, spiked landscape. There are mountains and valleys; the climb is slow, prolonged; the descent is swift, perilous. At last on level ground, we pass abandoned cars, rusted machinery. Several times we notice the heavy birds circling above a dark mound, a weighted presence in the dust-filled air.

Stopping at a small village to slake our thirst, we move through a row of hooded, sweat-stained faces. We discover the focus of their attention—a smudged notice tacked to the wall: news of an ambush, a flood, other disasters—and recall the gray bird that found death on our windshield, other things that filled the sky that deep, wet night.

8.

We reach our destination: a village in the mountains recommended by our friend. In contrast to the landscape we have passed through, there is a lake and tall, sheltering trees. The nights are cool. We find several here who speak our language. (None of them has "crossed over.") After a few days, we decide to remain. In the time that follows, we take short trips into the surrounding countryside. Occasionally we attend a party or a picnic. We grow accustomed to the faces, the weather. We live through various illnesses.

There are nights when we cannot sleep, mornings when we wake to the shriek of a slaughtered pig. And always those dark brown things that crawl through the cracks in the tiled floor—sickness and death in their sting.

And there are also festivals.

*

Reading the above, it is clear that not enough has been said about those moments that immediately precede the crossing. For so much then seems to weigh in the balance: all we leave behind, whatever we are going toward. We already sense what is on the other side: a place where expectations are irrelevant and have no connection with reality.

*

It is this that echoes again on another continent, perhaps a decade later. (Can it be that long?) Once more we approach the border. Surely this time, considering all we have lived through ... We hand the green-uniformed guard our passports. He turns the pages, compares the small, glossy square with eyes, mouth, color of hair. We notice the thick leather belt, brass buckle, polished boots. (Will he be the one to discover who and what we are?) The white-gloved hand waves us on ....

*

It is possible, of course, that we have missed something. That we have not yet learned to make the crossing as it should be made. (Consider those who cross not once, but twice during a single day.) We are not, after all, smugglers, nor have we ever been in the pay of a hostile power.

Yet we cannot help wondering: Was it ever possible for us to be at home with those bright-colored birds, those rich pure flowers? To understand those voices that cried so hard and sang so loud— in one strange language after another?

1966/1970

Leaving the City

Time to get out of the city! With all that's been happening, it's no surprise to be hearing this again. The only difference this time is being told it's not necessary to travel a great distance. A day's drive, they say, is far enough. We can head north along the coastal road to where the population thins out. (In the few far-between towns, there are often only a few hundred inhabitants.)

And what do I think about all this? It's hard to leave friends, treasured objects, the charm and excitement of the city. And for some it may prove impossible. For those able to make the choice, I recommend a location near where a river enters the sea. (About a hundred miles north, there are a number of such places.)

The suggestion is made because on days when the coast is bleak and fog-covered it is often clear just a few miles inland. The places I have in mind are easily accessible, with paths to follow, beaches to rest and picnic on. One can lie on the warm sand, listen to the wind in the dry stiff grass. One note of warning however: be alert to what happens in the sky. The presence of certain birds, the portent of a wandering cloud, needs to be kept in mind.

For the fact is, having lived so long in the city, we may have some difficulty separating promise from menace. And because of this we may fail, at some essential moment, to distinguish the Vulture—the dreadful image—from the majestic circling of the unimprisoned Hawk . . . .

1979

Part Two: The Watchers / The Watched

*"We have learned then to be careful, to examine the faces,
listen for a word, an accent that does not belong here."*

"Trying to decipher what moves faster than the eye, the mind."

The Invaders

1.

There was a time when they appeared at a distance: poised on the hill in perfect ranks, armored, helmeted, spears glinting in the sun. Everyone considered then what it meant to be besieged. No one considered himself especially vulnerable, singled out by fate. Those legions were sent where the land was green, the vaults and coffers filled, jewels and women ripe for the plucking.

But as I say, that was a long time ago. We still wonder at the recollection: how simple it all was! For since then we have seen worlds falling—sometimes by assault, sometimes for no apparent reason. And the common view today is that the enemy has moved within the gates, taken up permanent residence among us. We have learned to be careful, to examine the faces, listen for a word, an accent that does not belong here. We have of course no idea where they might have come from, what their intentions are. But it is felt they could be walking among us—the disguises subtle, not easily pierced.

2.

. . . Moving from one room to the next in this small apartment, I keep turning up evidences of one or another unexplained presence. Just this morning, for instance, I opened the closet door: hanging there were suits, jackets, shirts—different styles, sizes, and colors. I had no idea where they came from, whom they belonged to.

And the same thing a couple of days ago when I looked into the kitchen cupboard. Filling the shelves was a fantastic variety of herbs and spices. As I read the exotic labels, I was struck by the irony: I do my own cooking, prepare only the simplest meals . . . . Why not throw out all this stuff? So says the naïve voice that always seeks an easy solution. But a moment's thought reveals the complications inherent in the real situation. To mention just one: the different views at different times. Thus I have to admit this is only clear to me—as right now—when I can see it with my own eyes.

For at other times, I could be standing at that same closet door, hand on the glass knob, and everything would appear in order. I could reach in, take out one of the shirts, put it on, and only later, while passing the mirror, become aware this was obviously not mine. (Never would I have purchased these garish stripes, this fancy silken material!)

3.

Why persist in these fantasies and self-deceptions? I know perfectly well there are no strange garments, exotic foods. I must stop playing these silly games—or risk never coming to grips with the real situation. To set the record straight: I have, it seems, invented these "appearances" and "disappearances": there are no "uninvited guests." And my reasons for this elaborate charade? Perhaps simply because it is more interesting to have all this going on. And I suppose it also helps to account for what is a genuine difficulty in maintaining my own presence, keeping things in order. (In a time like this, occasional "absences without leave" become necessary.)

Once this is admitted, it becomes possible to describe the experience: (1) I am standing "right here," speaking in my own voice; (2) for no apparent reason I begin to "drift off"; (3) I find myself "somewhere else," listening, watching what is going on. To borrow a familiar image: writing the play, watching the play, performing the different parts, all at the same time.

It is only when I question or reject the whole process—usually on the grounds it's too far removed from the rational view—that "the others" make their appearance. Clearly this happens because it is preferable to credit *them* with a separate existence, rather than regard the self as so many fragments. (Our number one article of faith: the whole greater than the parts.)

Looked at in this way, it all becomes harmless enough. I need not consider myself an exception: no one can be "himself" all the time. I have only to stop this insistence on living *my own* life, speaking with *my own* voice. The advantages should be obvious: the increased mobility, wider range of roles. I am wherever and however I appear. (Even in that silken, striped shirt!) And thus say goodbye to that fear of invasion, of displacement.

4.

None of this will do. These rational explanations all come to the same thing: by providing names and labels, they tend to make it all sound harmless, unimportant. All the torment, the sense of crisis disappears. What we have been subject to then becomes the result of some error, some defect of vision. So that one need only make an appointment with the nearest eye doctor, take the tests, find the proper lenses. One can then go forth upon these streets, between familiar walls, and find everything in place. No more blurring, no more distortions . . . .

5.

I seem to be back where I started. But with this difference: I have finally realized this must be happening all over the city. So there may be an obligation to share what I have discovered. It seems important then that I speak out, not remain silent. This would be with the greatest reluctance, since mine is not the temperament that seeks confrontation. Instead my natural tendency is to breathe the air of the present—whatever it may be—and to avoid public pronouncements. Yet one does not always have a free choice in these matters . . . .

6.

I wonder if, after all, some kind of compromise can be worked out. Is there some way of calling *them* to account, setting limits, clarifying where each properly belongs? But how does one get into a position where the authority to settle these matters can be invoked? The minimum requirement would seem to be that kind of presence and appearance which "the others" would be forced to recognize.

It would be simpler of course if one could honestly speak of and believe in the existence of "the enemy." We could rely then on the military metaphors: strategy, tactics, logistics, etc. The struggle would end in either victory or defeat; we would then be forced to arrange a truce, cease fire, draw up some sort of treaty. As it is, we continue to flounder, unable to resolve anything.

7.

To be silent—or to speak out? I would be willing to take a stand, but I know how easily my words could be distorted. At a time when public statements are suspect, it seems clear that anyone who steps forward will be subject to rigorous scrutiny.

Perhaps when the atmosphere is more favorable, certain steps might be taken. For instance, it might be of some value to reinstate the frontiers. After careful screening and selection, guards placed at all the known entrances. Of course, the gates would have to be locked, and an especially strict vigil kept on dark nights. We do not want to be unduly harsh in these matters, yet in order to maintain peace and stability . . . .

1967/1970

The Situation Room

1.

We sit facing rows of brilliant machines, trying to decipher what moves faster than the eye, the mind. Our fingers, agile from long practice, reach for the buttons, the small switches. A series of intermittent dots, broken lines, flash across the molded screens . . . This, we are told, is an exercise, a low-level alert. Another name for it is "the game," in which we simulate what has so far been called unthinkable. In this room, we are fairly low in the chain of command; we do not make decisions. Instead we separate "possible" from "probable," so those above us can select or discard. . .

2.

With all our training, it is still hard to accept: the games are over. We learn this when the light above the metal door turns red. Our attention now is centered on a huge electric map, which pulses and glows, articulating the target areas. . . . *Calls coming in:* rumors that we are, or are not, going to land in the desert. Outside I suppose there is still day and night, regular breathing, personal concerns. . . .

3.

Staring at a trajectory of swirling lines that streak across the map. A voice within says: time to forget before and after. Armed men are already on their way, moving toward the zero boundary. Men in jumpsuits, faces and hands smeared, are prepared for the leap, the dark visitation. . . .

4.

On the desert the night has almost ended. Whirling blades create a hover-motion; in a slow wobble, the craft descends. . . . And we who are waiting, watching, *what* are we? An inner voice responds that we are what we worship. When the news comes of the colliding machines, the failure of the mission, we tell ourselves: we must build new and better altars. . . .

1980

The Retreat of the Leaders

With the whole world looking on, there are limits as to what can be achieved. For whatever takes place in public view becomes, inevitably, a performance. Yet there are grounds for believing that, while staying out of sight and in close contact, something can be accomplished.

Here, the setting and atmosphere at Camp David can play a decisive role. Within the confines of this historic retreat, our leaders may reflect, not only on immediate concerns, but on the surrounding environment. On their walks, whether conferring or relaxing, they may observe the testimony of trees, plants and animals—direct evidence of what is endangered. And with the presence of these more profound influences as incisive reminders, we may breathe easier. For we too have walked along similar paths, shared the feeling of an enduring order . . . . *Retreat:* the word itself echoes. We recall those who went into the forest, not only to meditate and reflect, but to live. And at times in areas where life could only be sustained with berries, herbs, edible plants....

*

I have to record now—while hoping it is temporary—a feeling of disappointment. This follows our leaders' much-publicized excursion to the nearby Gettysburg battlefield. News photographs show the three of them on the summit of the historic hill, looking out across the scene of conflict. It was just here, we remember, that the Gray charged the Blue, and the nation wavered, almost split apart. (*Retreat:* an order given by a commander, usually in the face of a dangerous or hopeless situation.)

*

What happened at that moment when they stood—larger than life, if we believe it—above the visible, contained space of a miniature war? Were they frightened, or exhilarated, by the limited scale of destruction—the heritage of battles where the dead still had names and could be counted?

Whatever the answers, we cannot help wondering what makes them appear so content, even pleased, posing beside the polished barrel of an antique cannon.

(*Retreat*: going to the edge, then pulling back, after a brief glimpse of the Abyss.)

1978

The Leopards / The Temple

> *"Leopards break into the Temple and drink to the dregs what is in
> the sacrificial pitchers; this is repeated over and over again; finally it
> can be calculated in advance, and it becomes part of the ceremony."*
> —Kafka

1.

Not knowing the language of the original, I stare at the words,
which by now have an aura of autonomous existence. What can I
add that will not disturb their equilibrium? But I must not attach
too much importance to my own reading. These fragments,
after all, have a way of *floating* through our history: Archilochus,
Heraclitus, etc. Century after century the hand, the eye, exam-
ines them, finds something interesting, intriguing, then sets
them aside, turns toward something else.

2.

How poorly I read; how seldom I see beyond the surface! I re-
member the sociological rendering, which once seemed essen-
tial. The Leopards, I thought, are at first viewed as fearsome
invaders. But then it is realized that—as fear can be mastered by
desire—their return can be manipulated. Measures are then
taken to convert their rage into useful energy, bringing it into
service of the Establishment . . . . Of course, this appears now as
simplistic—a small first step toward unraveling . . . .

3.

Before going on I need to express thanks to a number of friends,
particularly to J., to P., to R. With their patient help, I have begun
to sense the myriad possibilities within and beyond the words.
One direct result is that I have looked closely at the word *pitchers,*
separating it from the word *sacrificial.* Thus I have been able to ask
the necessary questions: (1) What are the pitchers *made of*—glass,
pottery, silver? (2) What do the pitchers *contain*—blood, water,
wine?

4.

Do the Leopards in fact *break into* the Temple? This would imply the doors are locked and guarded. Yet more likely the doors are open; the Leopards *wander in*, are as astonished, bewildered as the Congregation. As for their return—"over and over again"— how is this credible? (Unless induced by bribery, false promises, other forms of duplicity.) Note too how the original departure, as well as the dramatic entrance, is left as ambiguity. Is it going too far to suggest the subliminal effect is, finally, to change "ceremony" into "performance"?

5.

We may have to abandon this line of inquiry. Our scholars, priests and clerks, ingenious as ever, can undoubtedly make all this believable. Of greater concern is the continuing triumph of the strategy by which we subdue and obliterate the wild. For by now, with our advanced technique, it is not necessary to use "real" Leopards. (For that matter, the Temple itself may just as well be simulated.) Is it any wonder then that—whatever we desire or fear—we can no longer tell whether a Leopard, a Unicorn, or the neighbor's child, is even now standing before the door?

1978

Trading with the Enemy

There are subjects not to be talked about, secrets not to be told. In the outer world, we hear of spies, double agents, a whole collection of shadowy figures who commit intrigue and, at times, violent acts. In the personal realm, however, the secrets are more tenuous, elusive, affecting only a few. Looking closer, the picture changes. True, what is at stake here is often only an image, an idea of the self. But still, for the individual—as for the government—there is a sense of humiliation, betrayal . . . .

*

. . . Sorting out the damage from the last visit. Determined next time to take action, to make sure the *enemy* is barred, kept at a distance. But is this really possible? Experience shows that the determined "other," after some delay, can always gain entrance. But this suggests we are dealing with an intruder. More likely, we know, that it is someone we have invited, been especially close to. . . . How does it start? In obvious ways: a random encounter, a phone call, a letter. In a short while, not knowing exactly how it happened, there is an involvement. It seems then we have only to travel that short distance between desire and fulfillment. It is only later, in retrospect, that the mirrors, even the walls, tell a different story . . . .

*

The one we have invited, cared for. Yes, now I remember. I was at home that afternoon, listening to some music, feeling quite relaxed. When the bell rang I walked slowly—with no apprehension— toward the door. *Do you remember?* Remember that, even though the visit violated our agreement, I greeted you warmly? Said nothing that could have given offense. Yet in a few moments, you stood there shouting . . . . I ask now: Isn't there some way to avoid this? To find out, in advance, what has to be negotiated? For it is clear that, without compromise, there can be no reconciliation. Think about those things you could give up and still be . . . . On my part, I assure you, I would be more than willing to . . .

1980/1981

36

Caesar's Thumb

. . . Still pouring into the Stadium, leaving hardly room to stand. In a short while Caesar is to make an entrance, here at this festival, the games that honor the Gods. To some he may appear no different, no greater than the Senators who surround him. But for us, even at this distance, a special aura will radiate his presence. Arms extended, we await that moment when Caesar stands there. It is then that our combined voices will break loose, reach toward the sky. For with that shout, we are embraced, included within the whole known world . . . .

*

The picture fades—that is the scene, the particular image. But desire, stronger than memory, moves us to fill the empty space. We dream other occasions—with horses, bulls, flashing capes—the combatants elaborately costumed or naked to the waist under an intense white light. Or we gather under some emblem or banner to ask forgiveness, to exorcise the violent impulse . . . . Yesterday Caesar, the Pope, the General, the President. And tomorrow? Our need for spectacles, for embodiment, takes many forms. Sometimes we yearn for a single figure who connects an enclosed Earth, a limitless Heaven. At other times we turn toward some less imposing, less obvious power symbol. Recently, for instance, a short, squat religious leader, an overweight adolescent with vacuous eyes . . . . Well, says the cynical voice, the Stadium is *there*, it has to be filled somehow . . . .

*

Standing before the full-length mirror, I rehearse the gestures. First the welcome: turning this way and that so all may feel included. Then calming them down, orchestrating the emotion. The idea is to sense what is *out there*—and just at the right moment, letting it enter a little at a time, before sending it out again . . . . I raise my right arm, waiting for the impulse to decide which way the thumb goes. My arm stiffens; even in this empty rehearsal, I cannot complete the turn. . . . Whatever happens, the outcome must not be traced here, but to the general movement, the anonymous voices in the crowd. So that I cannot be blamed for either punishment or reward—not even if neutrality is called "abandonment," given the name, the image of indifference . . . .

1980

The Contest

1.

It is fortunate there is a deadline. Otherwise where would it end? Looking around the crowded room—clerks carrying sacks and boxes, sorters busy at the metal tables—I wonder how much longer we can handle the deluge of entries.

For days now I've been sitting here, examining the glossy prints —a few in color, but mostly black and white—trying to find some basis for a choice. We have been told only to look for something *memorable*. Yet is this part of the intention? I am reminded this is a competition: with entries offered to gain the prizes.

I stretch, shift my position, lean back in the chair. Images of the day, the season, the year, the decade—the hurried view of a succession of moments? Clouds, trees, shadows, traffic, the faces of children. Out of all this to select eight or ten whose force and value cannot be denied . . . . The stack beside me glitters; a pile of discards reflects from the floor. Once more I try to separate what seems posed, artful, labored, from what respects the eye. But there it is: once more my attention goes to what needs to be excluded. No wonder I have so little to show . . . .

2.

How does one get into a situation like this? In the usual manner I suppose: there is work to be done, an opening occurs, a name is mentioned. There is an initial interview—a Secretary, an Assistant—and if all goes well, personal contact with the Director. And if it gets this far and the contract is signed, then it is obvious no mistake has been or could have been made. Perhaps that is why no one has interfered or objected . . . .

3.

It is typical that, having reached this conclusion, within the hour a note should arrive from the Director. He wants to know—as I might have guessed—what is holding up my selections. And concludes with the polite question: Would I mind stopping by to let him know how things are going? Somehow, for the moment, I feel more relieved than upset. There is plenty of time before the deadline. And looking around, I imagine that none of my colleagues are in better shape: a huge pile of discards surrounds each of them as well.

I start to reach into the nearest stack, but instead open the drawer and remove—is this all?—two that I have set aside: a woman seated in a chair by an open window, a man leaning against a streetlight . . . . I was sure there was at least one more—yes, that one of the ship going down. I search through the pile on the table, sift through what has landed on the floor. Only then does it occur to me: it was in yesterday's batch. So of course it is too late: by now it has gone down the chute to be chopped or burned with the rest of the excess paper.

I close my eyes. There was the prow sticking up out of the water, gulls circling, a slash of moonlight. It brings back various ships on various seas, and that time when, close to the shoreline, the waters turned red . . . . I open my eyes: this kind of drifting can be dangerous. Perhaps I should resign. I should have realized that to dream and to act are opposites. Even more confusing when to act means to choose, to judge the value of another's dream.

4.

Waiting to enter the Director's office, I reread and study the note. It is on good paper, with neat margins, and the words are printed. It is disappointing not to have a sample of his handwriting, yet the small letters, the light blue ink must mean something . . . . The buzzing sound is repeated several times before the Secretary emerges, announces a delay. I relive the moments just before, passing through the Judging Room. For the first time I felt the presence of the others in a special way. A kind of complicity in that slight turn of the head, eyes raised and quickly lowered . . . . Can the chooser tell when he is chosen? I see now that my presence here is nothing but an embarrassment for the Director. Efforts of the kind I exert—or fail to exert—are precisely what interferes with the best intentioned of projects.

5.

. . . Good to be once more in motion, taking steps on stone, on grass-covered ground. Pleased my vision has not been affected, that I can look at what is here without having to judge, to evaluate, part of that whole mechanism that offers rewards—or confirms obscurity. Pleased too the Director accepted my resignation in good grace, so that my failure here will not stand in the way of future employment in some other, more congenial capacity.

6.

Seated at my own desk, I open the large yellow envelope. (How was I able to get past the guards with so little effort?) This is what I have taken with me, a last-minute impulse, after leaving the Director's office: a small collection of images that represent a curved span of years . . . . The handle of a plow surrounded by a vast expanse of sand. A woman's name lettered across the side of a tank. A dark, plumed shape darting through the air. The pock-marked sphere itself, turning in wild, blue space . . . . I squeeze the envelope into an already overcrowded drawer, and, closing it, make the usual resolve to some day organize its scattered contents . . . . What I need to know is that I have been where I have been. I could look inside, take out the personal albums—and beyond these, letters, folders, schedules. But what would that prove? That I have set foot in the river, swimming sometimes with the current, sometimes against, other times floating easily in the sun . . . . I am not sure whether to laugh or to weep. Images of burning buildings, of snow, of waters on the rampage. Then suddenly in the center of a peaceful town, the stone steps of a Courthouse . . . . No need to ask who sits there, or in what capacity. Consider instead those darting figures ready with shutter and lens: future contestants.

What prizes then for the eye behind the eye? What rewards for the quick fingers—bent just that much—that unite memory, as evidence, with precise and unfailing judgment?

1980

The Cage: The Performance

Sharing the common darkness, we wait for the figure clothed in light to appear. We have seen M. many times before: the incredible body moving through space, presenting a world we imagine but can never express. With affection and admiration, we recall his performance as Clown, as Tramp, as Lover, bringing a kind of delight we thought lost, reserved for children . . . . But tonight, mixed with our anticipation, there is also a certain uneasiness. This centers on a work being premiered, with the disturbing title "The Cage Inside the Courtroom." The program refers to it as an update of an earlier piece, using images from recent political events. . . .

*

Watching the lithe body, with its stark counterpoint of black tights and whiteface makeup, we do indeed begin to feel the enclosed, stifling space of the Courtroom. Without props and without words, the scene starts to emerge: the uniformed men on guard, the terrified spectators, the machine-like exchanges between Prosecutor, Judge, Lawyers for the Defense. And finally the Defendants pacing the floor of the Cage: the curious gestures of those who are both threatened and threatening. . . . With the performance reaching its climax, we have a sense of the Defendants *clawing* at the bars. But then, very subtly, we are shown the other side of this—as though the "clawing" is being replaced by "stroking." The Cage then appears as not only a prison within a prison, but also as "home" or even "nest." And it is as though, with this shift from outrage to languid unconcern, the verdict has already been rendered.

*

As it turns out, we may have somewhat misinterpreted M.'s intention. For what is going on now, with the Defendants having subsided, the Cage itself fading into the background, suggests more of a game than a shrill reality. What we sense now is the Magician at work, letting us know this too can be dissolved, made to disappear, but strangely also—how to say this?—a kind of pedantic Lecturer sketching and erasing on the invisible blackboard a series of indecipherable equations.

*

The faces in the lobby tell more than the applause. Leaving the theatre, they seem more perturbed than pleased. As though with all the admiration for M.'s consummate skill, there is also a certain resentment. With this response, we should not be surprised if this too—like the earlier version—is dropped from the repertoire.

For as a shrewd judge of what will and will not "play," M. knows there is no substitute—no matter how interesting or daring the experiment—for material that can "captivate" an audience. Even in a medium that, presumably, extends beyond the barriers of language.

1978

The Actor: Farewell & Return

for George Hitchcock

1.

Waiting for the applause, for a moment he feels nothing is going
to happen, that a wall of silence is about to descend. He tries to
shrug it off as the vague residue from some untraceable dream . . .
As the sound reaches him he exhales, relaxes. Then starts the
practiced bow: to the left, the right, the center . . . . It is time, he
thinks, to say goodbye. Goodbye to all this light and noise. But
he is not yet ready to make the necessary move. Something needs
to be solved, to be remembered. But what is there, beyond the re-
cited words, the costumed character? He breathes deeply,
shakes loose from the reverie, and at last in motion, begins the
practiced exit. Slowly then, with every nuance of that borrowed
authority, he makes his way offstage.

2.

In this cooler, darker place—hanging ropes and stored scenery
—he leans against a curved facade and waits. The sound is less
than desired, but more than feared. With an unconscious mo-
tion, he raises his arm, holds the watch close to his ear. Someone
approaches, whispers a few words, walks away. The applause
begins to fade; it is the difference between enthusiasm—lightly
motivated—and passion. It seems that is indeed all—all there is
going to be . . . .

3.

In the dressing room, rows of short-stemmed bulbs frame the
mirror. For a while he sits there staring at the glass. Then he dips
his fingers into the open jar and rubs the thick cream over his face
and neck. Wiping it off, he squints and scowls, makes faces at his
changing face. With a sudden motion, he stands, sheds the rest of
the costume: the brocade, the sash, the satin-edged pants. At the
moment of nakedness, there is first a feeling of relief then—in
quick succession—chills, panic, and a feeling of confidence . . . .

44

4.

Approaching the door that leads to the street, he stops, unable to continue. He feels the pull, the pressure of unfinished business. He turns, retracing his steps, back toward the stage . . . . All at once he is there, feeling awkward, strange, in his street clothes, alone in that huge, empty space. Why has he come back? His hands and lips begin to move . . . .

5.

. . . Now that it is being said, he can express regret for past performances—on stage and off—that evoked facile loves and naïve hates. (While under the mask or makeup, the feeling of nausea was barely held in check.) Well, now that he is leaving, he confirms that none of this was meant to be taken too seriously. For the fact is that, moving out into the formless world, he has no magic or arms with which to defend himself. Instead, where his presence *as himself* is required, he faces predicaments for which there is no plotted outcome . . . .

6.

The dark, the single light dissolve; the theatre warms to his gestures, his soundless words. He stands for another moment, testing the air, waiting for the voice: *Speak, speak now, but only as yourself* . . . . He is left with this and nothing but this. And so he says aloud: *As you are, I am myself* . . . . And with this there appears row after row of flowering faces. Here, there, everywhere, bringing the gift of their responding hands . . . . At last he turns, moves off the stage. Nothing can stop him now. Carried along on this warm current, he can go forth upon those anonymous streets, taking with him those lively, lovely hours of pretense.

7.

Let us assume then that he finds as much to dream about in this ordinary, actual world. That here too entrance and exit can be as easily arranged as where whispered cues underline the action . . . Move then where he moves; stand where you can see his many selves joining hands, forming a lively, colorful throng. Who are those prancing figures dressed in velvet, striped silks, wearing painted masks? We can guess or imagine according to our fancy. For as we watch, it seems their antics—*vivre* and *survivre*—could indeed transform the very air.

1973/1980

The Trouble with Winds

The winds arrive; the winds descend. At first we feel grateful, released from the oppressive, stagnant air. It is only later, as we observe the direction and the greater force, that we become concerned.... This then is how it might happen: a day or two of advance notice, to which some respond. But thousands, hundreds of thousands, are too preoccupied (and with what?) to pay attention. For these even a hurricane, an earthquake, is somehow to be lived through, evidence of a will or pattern beyond their control.

*

I have been watching, listening to the news. A month ago winds twisted through the Midwest, leaving whole sections of cities as scattered debris. More recently, a hurricane swept across the peaceful, musical islands south of here .... Once more the images of dazed survivors: an old man wandering among the remnants of a house, a child holding a headless doll, a cat crouched inside a bathtub....

*

If we could trust the instruments, the experts, we could still carry on the ordinary business of living. We could continue using our voices, the known words, to verify our existence. Instead we have begun listening for a "voice" within the wind. Various governments have even installed huge metallic "ears" in strategic places.... Can these ever bring the message—if not redemption, then at least some possible reprieve? Or when finally heard and deciphered, will it be nothing more than the report of worlds shattered and renewed—aeons before our earth was formed?

1980

Part Three: The Codes / The Signals

"What then is this: some magic in the gesture, in these particular hats? Is the nod, the slight bow, a sign of mutual recognition— of a secret brotherhood?"

"Forgotten also those fantasies of the knock as 'signal' to the one inside: lover, confederate, secret agent."

The Hat, The Indian, The Lizard

> *"Neither an Australian bushman nor an ancient Greek could be*
> *expected to realize that the lifting of a hat is not only a practical*
> *event ... but also a sign of politeness."*
> —Erwin Panofsky

1.

An Indian stands watching as two men, moving toward each other, raise their hats, nod and go their separate ways. The hat, he thinks, is to cover the head, protect it from sun and wind. What then is this: some magic in the gesture, in these particular hats? Is the nod, the slight bow, a sign of mutual recognition—of a secret brotherhood?

2.

An Artist is in his studio painting the portrait of an Indian. The Indian is in formal dress: jacket, pants edged with black satin, a white silk shirt with ruffles and pleats. Completing the outfit, the hat is of a kind once worn by bankers and presidents . . . .

3.

This painting is now finished. I have just received notice it is for sale. At the price asked, I can recommend its purchase: in years to come, it is bound to increase in value. I should mention, however, that it is not a "pretty picture." For one thing, the Indian appears as more confused than noble. Also that, for reasons beyond me, the Artist has draped a fierce-looking lizard across the Indian's shoulders.

4.

Can we come back now to the original situation? Only this time, to clarify matters, let us stand on the street. Witness now the exchange as two or more—man, woman, or child—approach. Notice that, even without hats, there is some gestural wave or nod. . . . Is this too familiar, too trivial for comment? Note what it signifies: no harm offered, no fear evoked.

5.

For contrast we might recall the scene from a recent film: twilight on a deserted beach; from behind a cluster of rocks a shadowy figure emerges . . . . No need to fill in the details; we have imagined this or some variation a thousand times. That is, we have felt the one coming toward us as the source of mistrust and danger. So that even without the hat, the Indian, or the lizard, we still need some icon or amulet to protect us from the other.

*

I have tried ending the parable here. But private memory wants to add something to social memory. I move past a series of barriers, retrieve the title of a long-forgotten poem: "The Survivors: A Legend." The West as dream, as myth, as lost reality. A few lines return: "Beside the painted bodies of the slain/ Dust rises where the lizard's quick tail / Scatters the loose pebbles."

The primitive, someone says, is never far away. No matter how often we change our icons, our styles of clothing . . . .

1980

The Given Day

1.

We choose the time—or the time chooses us. Whichever way it is, encounters, events only signify in retrospect. While it happens, things simply follow one another: the faces, the names, the places drifting past.... The first day of W.'s last visit. Thinking of it now, it centers on that silly errand to City Hall. Imagine, the new rules require a Visitor's Permit, which for some reason is available only at the Tax Collector's office.

2.

Early afternoon, a bright, warm day. Approaching the building, we are both in a good mood, though irritated at having to waste time in this way .... We enter, moving past the security guards, the metal detectors. Crossing the stone floor, we pass a row of tables covered with booklets of various sizes and colors. This turns out to be part of a temporary exhibit: Keeping Your City Beautiful. Walking past we are each handed a blue plastic bag—a trash bag!—which we fold and stuff into our pockets .... W. has never been here before. When we come to the open space and the wide, stone staircase, he stops and looks around. I think he's going to comment, but he just shakes his head, shrugs, and we move on.

3.

. . . I fill out the form, pay for the permit. We are ready to leave, when I notice a familiar face. I introduce A. to W. "What are you doing these days?" "Well, I've just published a book." "I have too." We write the titles on scraps of paper. As A. leaves, I glance at the title: *Morality and Existence.* I wonder how to reconcile this with his offhanded reference to "some real estate venture" which he's just offered to account for his presence here . . . .

4.

... Crossing the street, W. notices the sign outside the Museum: Art and Geometry. I'm not very interested, but W. as a sculptor, architect, recognizes some of the names.... We spend an hour or so going from room to room. Occasionally, W. stops and makes a brief comment.... Leaving, I notice he seems depressed. When I ask, he says it's been happening on all his recent visits to museums and galleries. He explains it's not what's being shown, but the feeling of a kind of "packaging" that includes everything....

5.

We sit silently, driving through traffic. I recall our first meeting—on a day not unlike this—on a street in Rome. We were standing beside a fountain, looking at the gleaming statuary.... There is a sense of convergence when he speaks: "In time that staircase will take on a patina too."

6.

The staircase, the pseudoclassical interior. What makes the connection—the recent shooting there, the dim echoes of a falling Caesar? Whatever it is, my mind travels from the staircase to the corridor beyond, to that afternoon when the Mayor invites the distraught man into his office, then stops as the shots ring out—echoing and reechoing across the polished stone....

1981

The Career of Hands

Seated at the desk, I wait with hands poised above the keys. Usually I get a signal, a clue on how to proceed. This time, however, only some vague suggestions, impossible to follow. My choice then to lower the hands and make contact is arbitrary, without direction. But for a while just the sight of letters becoming words is reassuring....

*

... Under a shaped beam of light, I see the bench, the polished, curved wood of the piano. The stage is immense; the audience a silent, weighted mass. Coming forward I resist the impulse toward panic and flight. Since I am here, I tell myself, my destination is also my destiny. Yet I cannot be sure whether I am worthy of the instrument, nor whether I can perform the prescribed music....

*

... As I enter the crowded chapel, heads are turning, being raised toward the huge panorama on the ceiling. Bending back to look there, I find the familiar images of God and Adam somehow distorted, out of focus .... I turn then toward the walls, the curved arches that support the ceiling. What of the mason, the laborer, who put the stones in place? No clue as to what brings the urgent question. No possible answer. Above us the extended arms, the groping fingers, continue to miss connection. ...

1979

A Simple, Factual Report

1.

A curious item arrives in the mail. At first sight it appears a routine announcement: some poets giving a reading. But then I notice, below the names, a printed diagram. With this is a set of instructions—for some sort of computer—on how to deal with the human voice. If a "wrong" procedure is followed, the voice will be disregarded. If correct, the message will be received; then and only then will the proper circuits be activated . . . .

2.

A man with no voice is seated on the brown couch in our living room. He makes himself heard by a device—fitted into the palm of his hand—placed flat against his throat. At first the sound is unclear, the words barely recognizable, but then, listening closely, we are able to follow . . . . He is saying that the device was originally developed for use in animated films, to simulate speech for the "talking" creatures. He has been using it for the past few years, following an operation during which his larynx was removed . . . .

3.

He places before us a small collection of carved wooden dance masks. Their history, the myths, the symbols, are unknown to us. And for him, as a dealer in art objects, they are primarily items for sale . . . .

4.

What I am writing here is a factual report. Nothing is being added to color or intensify what happened. Why then the sense of struggle, of conflict, of fear? As if there were something forbidden about the mask—these particular masks. Vaguely we recall myths of spirits summoned and dismissed, of protection and exorcism.

5.

Disturbing echoes—yet we still insist on the need for fiction, for
ritual. This while it appears certain that the voice which strug-
gles with emotion, with meaning, is now obsolete. Already
available is a wide selection of devices, all of which are better
suited for the transfer of information. Becoming more and more
efficient, they are able to not only record what we say, but keep
what we remember in a safe, warm place.

1980

Reading the Text

From our part of the world, the effort to separate the sacred from the profane seems to require an elaborate system of taboos and prohibitions. Yet from the perspective of the *Mudra-Shad*—a copy has recently, after much delay and involved effort, come into my possession—these restrictions are irrelevant, even absurd. For as I read the Text, what comes across is a tolerance for whatever happens, for all human actions. This derives from a view of phenomena within some vast cyclical scheme of things. And while this may appear to Western eyes as random, chaotic, the Text itself offers evidence of design and pattern emerging *naturally*, according to the scale and time frame.

Thus, instead of the complicated structure of logic and reason, we are invited to partake of a universal vision. Central to this is the premise that, while what we do or fail to do may *irritate* the Gods, it does not call forth rage or vengeance. What we call "sin" is there regarded more as a matter of intrusion—in an area and at a time disturbing to the Gods, busy with their own concerns.

*

So far, we are still reading—in line with our traditions, our inheritance—with expectations of punishment and reward, following the metaphor of "rise and fall." And while seeking, I might add, not merely equilibrium, but something more extravagant. I refer of course to our numerous myths of death and resurrection.

What the *Mudra-Shad* offers, however, is in the more modest realm of transformation. This means putting aside our yearning for an accessible heaven, in favor of a "renewal" in which another, but still earthly form is assumed . . . . An equally important difference, revealed as I turn the pages, is how the metaphor of Water takes over the role we ascribe to images of Light. So that where we refer to "radiance" as reflections of Supreme Being, the Text speaks of a "current" within the flow of things.

*

How curious then—and how confusing!—to turn from this to the "dry world" of our own sacred texts: dust returns to dust. Or when we read the words of one of our poets: "fear death by water." This in contrast to the opening lines of Book One: "In water we began. In water we continue." *Remarkable* when we consider these lines were composed by monks dwelling for centuries in almost total isolation—a few thousand feet below the peak of an almost inaccessible mountain!

*

Further comment at this time seems needless. The *Mudra-Shad* is a text no scholar or generation of scholars can adequately render or transcribe. Like any eternal work, it appears differently in different times and places . . . . With all this said, I regret that, due to the enormous labor, the difficulty of transportation, it is impossible to tell when additional copies will be available.

1978/1979

The Master

Of course the birth took place. For those whose interest centers on this, there are documents, witnesses and so forth. I have held in my own hands volumes in which the circumstances are described—and in such fashion as to convince all but the most biased and self-seeking. One such volume I recall with a thick blue binding, on good paper, and with a number of clear, detailed photographs. Others I have looked at appear well researched, comprehensive in their presentation of the facts.

But I learned long ago that the real interest of all these scholars, critics, commentators was in something beside the facts. This happened when I first came across the phrase "born of the cruellest of fathers." The writer's name, understandably, has been forgotten, but the sentimental and misguided intention—which put me on guard for what followed—has remained. For it was the starting point for a whole school of would-be analysts, making careers out of what their probing fingers pulled apart.

I will not put either that life or those words under that harsh, searing light, but will repeat what is beyond dispute, that the birth took place. And add a few words, not to explain anything, but to express my feeling about a presence that changed the course of my existence.

*

I am sometimes asked to comment on how it is that this terrible gift and burden appears so incredibly close to our own time. And yet, as one considers it, it could not have happened any sooner. One realizes that somehow it had to be in just that country, and after those particular wars. One cannot help thinking of those tidal waves which, in their own time, reach the intended shore. Or to change the figure, of molecules already in the air, seeking the body they have to enter. Whether others would go quite that far, I cannot tell. But there should be little disagreement on the force and significance of his presence. I have to call it a great "dividing line"—one of the greatest. Let those who would dispute this only look at their morning paper; let them take the shortest walk on our endangered streets. That is where they may test the clear-sightedness of his prophecy—on those destroyed faces, in the vague eyes of wandering, mindless children.

I am tempted to say the obvious: *his children.* For who else understood so well the role of corridors, of endless desks placed side by side? But it would not be accurate to present the prophecy that flowed through him as if it were, literally, the work of his hands. It was rather what he saw and felt and lived with—if we understand this in the proper way and in the proper dimension—as far as our own limited minds can reach.

*

With these few glimpses of what lies beyond, I am content now to take my place among his readers. His words are by now preserved in countless editions. Let those who read make of them what they can. They have the printed pages; they can use his name wherever and however they choose. What is missing, of course, is his voice. That was available for only a short time, and for those few to whom he gave so generously of his unique spirit. *His voice.* Those seated beside him at the same table . . . . The words go on; they flow through his silence. That silence which was his last considered choice. For wasn't it enough for them to know that he had been there; could they not have pooled their memories of his presence? But this was not to be. The hand of one closest and most trusted sifted through his papers; fingers tightened on sheets covered with black ink.

We have read those words—read and recited over and over again—and understood nothing. The experts still express astonishment that he could speak of the Garden as if he had been there in person. Some of them even revel in the opaque, counting the tiny prisms made with the points of their pens. They cannot grasp what goes deeper than their lives. Not a choice for darkness but for the earliest light: *before the forest awakens, before the intruder arrives.*

1970

The Sacrifice

He is there with a number of others—all of them articulate, concerned with words—trying to decide what can be said, what can be heard as intended. Their voices join, separate, dispute. He wonders, as always, where the voices come from, go to after leaving this privileged space.

Only recently he has had to record the impact of another death. This particular one, skilled in the manipulation of images, has died after an incredibly prolonged ordeal . . . . As the voices continue, he recalls the published account of his friend's death: with sight gone, with speech gone, there was still a choice for life. It was only when the man's *hearing* started to fade that the choice for death was made. He wonders then at the cost, the value of speech. Words as urgent and terrible as *knife, gun, axe.* Words to suggest the flesh deprived, destroyed . . . . It occurs to him that, over and over again, the sacrifice has been made. But the lesson—whatever it is—is quickly forgotten. For the strange part is that before the sacrifice, an offering must be made. And while sometimes this is acceptable—victim and martyr honored, later even worshiped—at other times it has been ignored, refused. More than this, if certain accounts are believed, it has been laughed at, ridiculed.

Someone beside him asks for his response to the words that have just been read aloud. He pauses for a moment, then answers with words appropriate to the question.

1978

Protective Measures

"We humans are held together by signals which move back and forth across our body, just as an army is held together by its messengers."
—J. McKim Malville

Almost a year has passed since our last meeting. And we still think of G.—whenever we do—in her role as teacher, rather than friend. For the fact is we are too busy, too concerned with immediate tasks to observe the obligations of friendship. And no regrets about this. Where nothing more is asked, or promised, no harm is done. Difficult enough to maintain ties with those close at hand, without expending energy on those far away. (G. lives in another country, returns here once or twice a year.)

*

How long must one live to apprehend the truth of things? Not just these things, but *any* things. For as I think of G., I wonder what we have in common. During her absence, for instance, what does memory visualize? No more than a vague image—the energetic, the "life-affirming"—a metaphor instead of a person. In this respect, she does come to mind more than the other distant ones. This happens when we perform the exercises—or *lessons,* as G. prefers we call them. And especially when we recite the simple phrases—"chest buoyant, fill the space with your breathing"—she spoke while her skillful, healing fingers probed.

*

I am still withholding something, offering less than the truth. For I have not yet admitted that these lessons stir resentment, the sense of participating in an absurd activity. What are we doing, I wonder, giving our bodies so much attention? As much or more than we used to reserve for a book, a painting, a piece of music. There is nothing, after all, the least enthralling in the simple process: taking in and expelling air. And if our bodies suffer, even disintegrate from the absence of this constant scrutiny, it will be because we are directed elsewhere.

1979

The Shrinking City

It is time to acknowledge openly what has already been verified by a number of independent sources: *our city is shrinking!* And this in spite of all efforts, especially in the past year, to further various "expansion" programs. These include raising the permissible height for new structures, as well as extending the city limits . . . . As for the reaction of our citizens, it is varied. Some still insist nothing has changed. Confronted with the evidence, they claim that it is our perception that has somehow been altered. Some have even suggested a temporary affliction, to be corrected by the compulsory wearing of special magnifying glasses.

All this brings us to a difficult point: is the same thing happening to us, the inhabitants? I refer now to my own experience: earlier this year I had already noticed the smaller size of the house, the furniture. One day, returning from work, I had to squeeze through the door. The next day, to my surprise, I was able to enter without difficulty. I decided to check my appearance in the full-length mirror in our bedroom: *there was no change!* It was only later that it occurred to me: of course, the mirror itself was now reduced . . . . This morning on my way downtown, I recalled the old saying, "Never a disaster, but someone benefits." Yet as I thought of it, who could that possibly be? An obscure item in the morning paper caught my attention: model makers, toy stores selling miniature houses, doll furniture report that business has never been better . . . .

1980

The Knock

"Kings do not touch doors. "

—Francis Ponge

1.

Thinking of what I am about to write, it is already clear how much has changed. That is, having settled into the role of the one whose door is knocked upon (clumsy as that sounds), I have forgotten those times when I stood outside, waiting for someone to respond. Forgotten also those fantasies of the knock as "signal" to the one inside: lover, confederate, secret agent—all actors in the drama of my younger days....

2.

Hearing it now, in this present time, I listen for a sound that signifies. Is it a demand or, more moderately phrased, more of an inquiry? Obvious that the light tap, compared to the urgent pounding, sets up a different expectation. Also that each caller has the *choice* of whether to knock or ring the bell. Some constant visitors—as I recall—make the same choice each time, but others, for no apparent reason, alternate between one and the other.

3.

The door is our front door, which opens on the street. Those who live at some height, whose doors open onto other doors, must have a different perspective. The image there is of numbered rooms along a narrow corridor, as in an apartment house or hotel .... Does anyone come knocking there? I imagine that the sound is becoming rare. Callers use bell or buzzer, are scrutinized upon a glass screen, or through a slotted opening....

4.

The intersection then of a need and a fear. We live in a time, a place, where each encounter is valued or rejected as it relates to one or to the other. With this in mind, the parameters of "good news" and "bad news" can be guessed, seen as predetermined.

And if this sounds vague, listen to the voice of another time: *Where I grew up, the doors were always left unlocked . . . .*

5.

Memory provides the counterpoint. Leads to another house, another street. To the child who, not long ago, came calling here. As I come to the door, see him standing there, I anticipate the words: *Do you have any cookies?* I open the door wider; he follows me into the kitchen. I reach for the container, lift the lid . . . .

6.

The view of the child, of the *as-yet-unrealized,* remains one of a continuing world, with all its difficulties, dangers. And of a door that can still provide a positive entrance . . . . The knock rather than the bell? It could be that. For however uncertain or peremptory, it proposes a sound unmediated, unchanged by connecting wires. The contact between flesh and wood may also, on some subliminal level, evoke a body as fragile, as endangered as our own.

*

There is a different way to treat this subject. One I would rather not think about, try to remember. It concerns knocking on a wall instead of a door. The sound there would be tentative, holding off desperation. Repeated a second, a third time, there would be more and more urgency . . . . When the response comes—the sound that tells us we are not alone—it would begin again. This time with a careful phrasing, the controlled waiting, and then the slow deciphering of a message we have never heard before.

1981

Part Four: The Myths/ The Emblems

"From here we may begin the decisive voyage: setting sail toward what is surely there."

"We still need this bright emblem to fill the dark moments of our empty, aimless days."

The Fifth Room

1.

For years we have heard there *is* such a place—in fact, there always has been. And I have been content to leave it at that: as an open possibility. After all, I am not one of those active *seekers* who, when the news reaches them, decide this is what they have been waiting for. Who prepares then for an arduous journey—ready for any sacrifice. But of course, if there is something at hand and the opportunity presents itself . . .

2.

At the invitation of a friend who works at the Museum, I arrive there early one foggy morning. As arranged, we descend to the basement, enter an area of packing boxes and dusty display cases. From one of these we remove a heavy, leather-bound portfolio. Inside are drawings of hooded monks, grotesque birds of prey. Moving across the black and white tiles of an immense room is a weird procession of chained animals, prancing gypsies, crippled children . . . .

3.

Months later I return for the widely publicized show: Forbidden Objects: The Underside of the Ancient World. At first it seems nothing more than what is advertised: instruments of torture, crude weapons, erotic art, etc. But as I drift through the eager crowds, the recognition comes. Could this be it, I wonder, could this be the *Fifth Room?* Yet why now, why here, is it being displayed openly?

4.

The show has closed after only a few days. For the first time in memory, the Authorities have found it necessary to issue a statement. It seems that, due to conditions in the countries of origin, the objects will have to be returned. A brief news report, however, reveals that the leaders of certain sects are claiming their most important shrines have been violated . . . .

5.

In the last few days, we have been inundated by competing voices. Some say that action, protest is called for. Others that this is futile, absurd: the exhibit was only a semblance of the "true space"—a harmless deception. Yet the clamor continues, with the argument that *any* display profanes what must, by its very nature, remain sacred and invisible.

6.

. . . Feeling more at peace now, having realized that all this will be resolved at some future time. It is for the others—those who come after—to decide. In this way Thought merges into Dream, raising Spirit beyond present boundaries to a wider horizon . . . .

7.

Are we in fact enclosed in a long, dark corridor? Or is there space, enduring space, beyond this? Surely this is the true question of the Fifth Room. For what is a place—or rather, what makes it for us *the* place? With so much pathos, so much longing, the names resound: Jerusalem, Alexandria, Athens, Byzantium . . . .

8.

It has come to me at last: it is not, as we were taught, some green paradise or moldy prison. But wherever we may approach and dream upon the visible shore . . . From here we may begin the decisive voyage: setting sail toward what is surely there . . . .

1980

The Message / The Messenger

It has been told so well, so definitively, that many of us still sit by our windows, waiting for a Messenger who never arrives. From this it is clear that Kafka, as teller of the tale, has indeed outdone himself. For his own "message," far from being lost or dissipated, continues in our consciousness. And to such an extent that the symbols by which he resonates that remote imperial world carry forward into our own frenetic age. Thus, we have not yet been able to admit that the King no longer dies—or if he does, no one pays attention to his dying words. The sad fact is that the King's death has become a statistic: as quickly, easily forgotten as any other.

*

How then explain the persistence of Kafka's "An Imperial Message"? Is it simply nostalgia for a time when, it seems, a few words could explain and resolve matters of the highest urgency? I believe it is more than this. For we have now available to us—by instant transmission—news of anything that happens anywhere. Speakers and listeners have become close as brothers, as lovers even, across the vast spaces of our planet. Yet through this enormous outpouring of speech and noise, data and opinion, we feel further apart than ever before.

*

It is clear that as long as we remain passively at the window, we only perpetuate the legend of the Castle, the stalwart, futile Messenger. It might be said, then, it is time we found another location. Not an easy choice to make, since it requires we leave this entrancing view, so close to the seething life of the streets. Besides, such a move, while it might benefit some, leaves out of consideration those who continue to dream of the dead King. I know of one, for instance, who dreamed only recently the King was still alive. They met in a garden and, for an hour or two, strolled hand in hand among the lush plants and graceful flowers.

*

Also to be considered is that—in Kafka's version—the Messenger is signified with the symbol of the highest authority—nothing less than the Sun itself!—glittering on his chest. And while we have no solid evidence for a witnessing of this triumphant image, it connects with countless examples from religion and mythology. (I should note: both those that encourage us and those that warn us not to dream this far.)

It seems certain then—even without the Messenger, or even the King—we still need this bright emblem to fill the dark moments of our empty, aimless days.

1978

Angel in the Freezer

One room in our house has a wall almost completely covered with painted wooden dance masks. I need not say, since it is outside the purpose of this narrative, how all these were acquired. But in order to not create a mystery, some were purchased years ago on our travels, some from a dealer only recently. Of the latter, two were obtained at a greatly reduced price: an Angel and a Devil. The dealer offered these for less because the wood was infested with tiny worms. I remember how we hesitated, wondering whether to accept his assurance that the problem was easily solved: a few days in the freezer and . . .

*

I have just been looking at the recently published *Book of Masks*. I am disappointed that, while several others are pictured there—the open-mouthed Jaguar, the woman's head surrounded by snakes—there is no representation of our Angel, our Devil. I will try then to give some sense of their appearance. The Devil is pink and brown, somewhat demonic, though not enough to inspire any real fear. The Angel, whom we have placed in the far corner, is more imaginative and surprising. The figure is definitely male, with a thick, black moustache. The face suggests a peasant prototype, like those that appeared so dramatically in Eisenstein's *Thunder over Mexico*.

*

Why am I telling this? Is it the "symbolic evidence" implied by the display of our very own Angel and Devil? This does seem to have awakened old feelings about dealers and collectors. Not only the greed, self-indulgence, but the offense committed by placing the sacred object in profane hands. I know, of course, that is not quite the case here: it is likely that whatever we own was never intended for any more than the marketplace . . . . Thinking it over, it occurs to me that something else is involved. Freezing the Angel, the Devil, saves them from the garbage can. And yet, and yet, if this was their destiny, how did we dare to interfere?   1980/1981

Reading Borges

For years I avoided reading him. Then one day, at the urging of friends, I read a few of the parables, the shorter "fictions." I saw at once how one could become intrigued with that intricate vision, but also how easily admiration could lead to imitation. For even if controlled, there was still the dazzling example of "a world which somehow we are permitted to enter." ("Borges: The Strategy of Emergence," Jean Perrier, *The Enigma Review*, Fall 1972.) Perrier's phrase underlines the danger. Especially the word *somehow*, with its suggestion of an "entrance" into another realm—without knowing how we got there, how to manage the passage, the return....

*

... I have put aside the books, but the words, the images continue to resonate. If Borges is right, the Labyrinth is not myth or metaphor, but inescapable fact—even the central fact of our existence. The case appears at its strongest in the story of Pierre Menard, referred to as the "contemporary author" of another version of *Don Quixote*. (Somehow identical with the original!) As one tries to penetrate the intention here, what emerges is the view that—at some other level of awareness—individual creation is, at the same time, the property of the whole species. For as we look in that direction, who appears but Quixote himself: eyes glazed, the elongated, disarrayed figure crossing an endless plain. But notice also: the same Quixote we always expect to see! One cannot help wondering: if we could somehow erase the expectation, what then would appear? Perhaps a Quixote who is both *everyman*—forever subject to fantasy and illusion—and the *very man* whom Borges describes as "always unique, always unfathomable."

*

... It begins to appear that all this merely scratches the surface. Coming back to the same story, observe how, just as Menard replaces Cervantes, he is in turn replaced by none other than

"Borges" himself, who may very well be—we are led to believe—merely another version of the original Borges who set all this in motion. What then are we left with? More confused than ever, our minds turn back to the mythology (history?) of the Labyrinth itself. We summon the figures, repeat the names: Daedalus, Minos, Ariadne, Theseus, and of course the Minotaur . . . . But this too, we realize, has to be abandoned. For what Borges has done is to locate his central metaphor not in this remote world but in a structure that is almost too familiar: the Library!

. . . Moving past those endless shelves, we follow a *fragrance*, as it were, that both invites and repels. Taking another look at Perrier's commentary, I find this phrase: "Borges sees through the one who is seeing through." Somehow this is both comforting and disturbing. On the one hand, it makes clear our need to be recognized as more than image. But on the other, it brings into view the self-conscious architect who presents this sense of confinement. So that with all our admiration for the constructed Library / House, the soothing overtones of Shelter / Sanctuary, there is still the sinister paradox: Prison / Labyrinth . . . . We return then for assurance to our own travels, in and through our dreams. Moving through memory, silence, and reflection, we amplify a certain scene. Fixing the time and place, we select a certain summer, bending to our purpose the uncertain light: Staring through the train window, heading north that year . . . *Suddenly the Caribou, appearing in that untouched elsewhere, beyond dream and remembrance, as we rounded the turn* . . . .

1980

The Choice

1.

After all these years, the same room, same furniture. He stands holding back a corner of the drape, peering down at the quiet street. I wait for him to speak, knowing he will without turning, without raising his voice. *You have a choice,* he says.

So that too has not changed: the dry tone, the slight accent. I remember how it used to bother me: Christ, are we going through *that* again?

He moves away from the window, goes over to stand beside the bookcase. He pulls out a thick volume, holds it close to his face. What is it going to be this time? Buddha, Maya, Tetragrammaton, Mazda—something about the Quest, legendary figures rising out of the Sea? He puts it back without saying a word, sits down in the faded pink chair. Again, I anticipate the gestures, as he takes out that old brass key, begins turning it this way, that way.

2.

How long has it been? It doesn't matter, I suppose, except for the expense. A brief glimpse of a procession of mornings: my voice, his voice, the silences . . . . I feel the present silence gathering: could easily become one of those prolonged ones. And so I speak, as much for the sound: You think I'm ready? *I think it's possible.* How can I tell? *You can't tell—in advance.*

We talk this way, I suppose, having gone over the same ground so many times. I am to understand, for instance, that the "in advance" refers to the need for discovery, but there are "no guarantees, no immunity"—whether going this way, that way, or standing still. (All I can make of this, in terms of choice, is that it seems to exclude retreat.)

And what will I tell the others? He shrugs, puts the key back in his pocket. *You'll find something.* But it will be difficult, I insist. *Yes, it will*. His voice sounds far away; he seems eclipsed by the objects in the room.

3.

He has become more voluble, more animated. As though, having said this, something has been released. He is telling some tale about a man with a cart: there are the cows whose color changes, now black, now white, now something in between; the man's encounters with the people who live on the mountain; the adventures that come with the slow, difficult descent.... I can already tell how this one is going to end: the man returns to the marketplace (by this time almost thirty years have passed) and, unrecognized, takes his place among the friends of his youth. All is as it was, except that now he sees them differently: the butcher, the potter, the wineseller, the rugmaker, all clothed in radiance.

But as he talks, something else is going on. My mind travels a different route—this way, that way, with no stages, no direction, no view that puts it all in place. Everything seems here and there, arbitrary, interchangeable.

I try to work it out: what do I mean by "there"? I mean meadows, hawks, shepherds, temples. And what do I mean by "here": lost streets, crippled dogs, store windows and newspapers, tabletops guaranteed not to burn, etc. And it is with these my days are filled. So that while it may be valuable to have that "panoramic" view, it is the immediate with which I have to deal....

He gets up, starts pacing the floor. Clearly he is disappointed at my lack of response. (I'm surprised how tall he is—never realize it until he stands, begins that back and forth motion.) Finally he returns to the window, continues in that low voice, again as if speaking to himself. And I listen in the same way, attention fading in and out, coming back, hearing it chime in my head.

4.

It is almost time to leave. My mind is filled with echoes and images: persons, places, remembered, forgotten. I regret not being able to accept the myth; certainly it would make everything easier. But it is the surface appearances—no matter how shifting or transient—with which I am most familiar. And at last this seems to reach him; for after another brief exchange, we are again mired in silence . . . .

Images of childhood; the usual inflated fears, the distortions associated with those dark places. All this sharply intersected by equally vivid images of old age: at eighty his leg turned black, gangrene; he began regularly to wet the bed; one day he bit an attendant. . . . Something begins to emerge: The Family Portrait. Look this way, toward the crawling child. Look that way, toward the crushed skin, the infected bone. Somehow this is what his words have evoked. It's hard to tell though if there's any connection.

5.

Is it possible a week has gone by? The usual absurd question. He looks at me expectantly. I plunge right in (to hell with those silences!) and make my report: dreams, streets, the office, the bed, etc. He listens, nods, waits for me to finish.

He reaches into his pocket, and it occurs to me it's rather soon for turning the brass key. But I look up startled as I realize it's a nail file. (And he actually begins filing his nails!) Our eyes meet for only a second—long enough to establish the transgression—and it is back in his pocket. He is again attentive and concerned. After the initial irritation, I'm prepared to dismiss it as a momentary distraction. And yet his next response, when it comes, makes me wonder . . . .

I can't imagine what brought this on, but he has started talking about himself, some recent events in his own life: his daughter's wedding, his wife's collection of seashells, plans for remodeling his house . . . . I suppose this sort of reversal does happen, yet it's extremely uncomfortable, being thrust this way into the role of listener. And if it had to happen, I cannot understand the choice of these trivial details . . . .

So we have lost it then—is that what it means? Yet I had felt we were at last coming close to what had to be said. I remember particularly the phrase "the grace of affliction." The way he stopped then, took a deep breath—as though having tried to say too much. For a moment then, there was a tone I'd never heard before, and the glance that asked an urgent question. All I can make of it now was that some kind of "commitment" was called for: by its very nature not to be named. Something I had to give up, without asking anything in return.

6.

We are back now exchanging words. And I find that I am missing the old silences. Is it possible that I have got it all wrong? That I have understood nothing about the climbing of the mountain, the return to the marketplace?

Yet I still feel that, in my case, this is not intended. In spite of everything, I seem to belong with those who are bound—over and over again—to make the small mistake. The journey then remains, as before, from here to there, without intentions and without reasons.

As far as the brass key is concerned, there are doors *not* to be opened. Not only then is it difficult climbing those rocks and gullies, but even those few stairs above and below the present level of my existence. I realize that I may never reach what lies scattered in the attic, stored in those cold cellars.

Yet aside from this, I am willing to let the light fall in whatever direction; spaces open and close where they can and have to; entrance and departure take place with neither sign nor announcement.

1970

The Loaves / The Fishes

1.

It's like a fish, he said, *a fish you're trying to fashion.* The voice on the phone said, *A fish?* Then after a pause added, *trying to fashion?* It had slipped out; he tried again: *not the real thing, but a semblance. As if you're working with clay, with dough.* Later in the conversation, he heard himself saying, *make up some small individual loaves....*

2.

Hours later, while shuffling papers on his desk, it suddenly struck him: the loaves, the fishes. What could he have had in mind? The words had come out while speaking of language, trying to say how one sought form and expression. It was a reminder, perhaps, from some unlighted, ungovernable source of a realm beyond intention. All very well, he thought, but then wondered what brought the metaphor of feeding—even feeding the multitude?

3.

He went through the day—another unremarkable day—before the thought returned. It came back as he recalled the party on the terrace . . . . It was years before in another country. A dinner served at twilight, in the presence of diving birds and gleaming statuary. The enormous fish was carried in on a silver platter. Carrot slices for eyes. The image focused to include cucumber wedges for scales, wavering lines of mayonnaise to represent the sea . . . . *Do we eat the words?* A mocking voice answered him, *In the beginning there was a loaf, a fish.*

4.

That night, in dream, he crossed the desert and reached the sea. On the shore he came upon a small group of kneeling figures. Coming closer he remained standing, wondering what it was that kept him apart. Under the bright sun and searing wind—as the stained robe stuck to his skin—he felt the hand that cooled and sustained them.   1979

The Dark Pattern

*"The shroud bears a dark pattern that appears to resemble
a crucified man."*

1.

What to make of this? A piece of cloth bearing an imprint, an
image. Something to be stared at, fingered in the mind. A brief
note from Q., which enclosed the clipping, suggested we might
go there and see for ourselves. But that would imply a certain
readiness, a certain predisposition. To go there properly—con-
sidering the hardships, the expense—wouldn't that mean to en-
roll in a kind of pilgrimage?

2.

Q.'s note has started a series of reflections. The obvious thing is
that a man lives, a man dies. Of this life—no matter how short or
long, fulfilled or meaningless—there are tangible and intangi-
ble reminders. The intangible emerge and recede in the flow of
memory; the tangible, as valued objects, are stored in a safe
place. Safe, that is, for as much as a lifetime. But after this, their
fate is questionable. We see them vanish in flood and fire—by
the hands of thieves, under the boots of a pillaging army.

3.

But what if it is more than a man—more than a King, or the great-
est of men? The flesh that was, we mean to say, has had its corpo-
real existence, has been incarnated with the divine. Is it appro-
priate, here also, to be concerned with tangible reminders?

4.

Consider the fragment of bone from the *sacred body*—this Saint's
toe, that Saint's finger—which draws throngs of the curious, the
faithful to certain cathedrals, certain shrines. Note that the rel-
ics are kept in vessels, often crusted with jewels, wrapped in gold
cloth—whereas the authentic thing, it seems, would signify its
own presence. Consider also the anonymous tin-paintings—
done within the past century—nailed to the outside walls: the

reverence of the poor. This in contrast to the image that acquires value because of the *image-maker:* the skilled craftsman, the great artist.

5.

Faith, said Paul in his *Letter to the Hebrews,* is without eyes. Is this view to be considered hopelessly antiquated?

6.

A long letter from Q. He says now that I've been taking the whole matter "too seriously." He quotes a recent book that claims, "Christ was one of a number, prevalent at the time, of magicians or mountebanks." Q.'s comment is that, while the tricks or miracles of the others died with them, Christ managed to perpetuate himself in a "marvelous, post-existence illusion."

7.

The news item in today's paper quotes two scientists with competing methods who have offered to analyze a tiny segment of the shroud. One of them is quoted as saying: if these were rocks being carbon-dated, wouldn't we be pleased at the addition to our knowledge? Why then feel so dubious, so uneasy about submitting a single thread to his laboratory?

8.

A man lives, a man dies. But that is not the end of it. There is need to solve the dark pattern, transform it into a source of light. The mind wants to finger what the hands cannot touch. So we summon that length of linen: soft, simple, stark enough to wrap the body.

But with that commitment to the tangible, we provide an opening for those marvelous instruments: letting *them* decide what is authentic. . . . Isn't it strange though—and even Q. with his "penetrating" insights has failed to note this—that the test would be conducted in the same laboratory where the atom was shattered? That the same technicians could be called on to verify the power of spirit—that otherwise we would always remain in doubt, not knowing which way to turn?   1978/1979

The Return of Sadhu

Sadhu, as he now calls himself, sits on a grass mat in a corner of the hut. Time for his rice and tea. I place cup and bowl beside him and wait for a word—a word that has yet to be spoken. He sips the tea, utters the fragment of a smile. Light touches the face and shoulders; the frail body is almost translucent.... I step outside, inhale the spiced air, the odors of morning. Beside me the familiar noises of the village—dogs barking, children playing—suggest a space confined, yet somehow limitless.

*

... Several months now since his return. More than a decade, I recall, from the day he disappeared. Not entirely gone from our lives, however. For besides memory and anecdote, there were the constant rumors. This or that traveler, passing through, saying they had seen or heard of him. These encounters, though, always in some remote area, under dubious circumstances....

... Who could forget the day of return? After raining all morning, around noon it suddenly cleared. I noticed the excited movement, the busy voices, the sudden rush of children drawn to that one place.... He has been with us ever since, a declining but still vibrant presence. We are so pleased to have him back, even with his new name, the enigma of what must have been an incredible journey.... Honored that having traveled so far, endured so much, he has chosen to live out his last days with us.... I have been particularly impressed by the spontaneous gathering, each evening, in front of his hut. It is then that he emerges, waves, smiles. He moves among us—venerable yet sprightly— touching and letting himself be touched. The gesture is playful and lighthearted on both sides. The touch I imagine is to prepare himself—and us as well?—not only for the coming absence, but surely also for the next return.

1980

85

Say We Are Going

"Ah, here it is: the distinguished thing!"
—Henry James
"Really my dear it is nothing, nothing at all."
—Italo Svevo

Say it is going to happen—as with these two—in a civilized manner. One has had this illness for some time and there is no remedy. One grows weaker, more confused .... The scene focuses on flowers in a blue vase. These are at first changed every day. Then, for reasons only too plain, every other day. In the last stages, the flowers remain until the petals are crimped and curdled. And so with the faces of the visitors: the expressions there too seem to shrink and wither, until signs of boredom transform the mask .... Forgive the hackneyed scenario. You may discard it, substitute something else from your own imagination. I would ask though that one version—on the grounds of personal distaste—be excluded. I refer to the scene in a novel (not by either of these writers) in which an old man falls, striking his head on the sidewalk. The psychologists will have no trouble with this: *the head is very important to you.* Yes, and it bothers me now because I have not said what I started to say: my love for both Svevo and James, encompassing the great differences between them. They both understood so much, wrote so well ....

1979/1980

The News from Dronesville

It may be only a habit of mind, an immemorial longing. But we invoke its existence as part of our own, as real as anywhere, anytime. By this process then—part memory, part invention—we construct the streets, the buildings. The Town, we tell ourselves, is now ready to be entered. The name, the location are not important; we need only be sure it's small enough, remote enough, to exist somewhere between sleeping and waking. . . .

*

. . . Children playing on the grass, old men and women seated on warped, wooden benches. Entering at the town square, we stroll through the small park which serves as focus, as center . . . . A warm day, almost without wind. Moving through the scene, we have for once the advantage of invisibility. Perceiving without being perceived, we could take our place beside any of these. We could be holding that newspaper, staring at the sun, or chasing that pink balloon. Part of whatever it is that intensifies the light, the shadows, the greenness of the grass . . . . For a moment, though, our mood changes as we view the discordant alternatives: the hurrying, not-seeing faces of the nine-to-five world. . . . The brief shadow disappears. We return to the scene as it was, as we want it to be. We feel confident enough now to even improve things. Our first choice is to add a statue: some benefactor or minor hero, the inscribed name suitably obscure. And next to it perhaps—why not?—a bronze cannon with intricate decorations. . . .

*

. . . Yes, we have chosen well, avoiding the temptation to convert peace into somnolence. We retain here the emanation, the fragrance of a world that reconciles the best of dream and waking. It can do no harm, in any case, to call attention to this neglected realm. For it is just here, where we assumed there was nothing more to learn, that we suddenly encounter the most appealing. . .   1980/1981

87

The Trial of Two Cities

1.

The argument went on for so long, reached such intensity, we feared it might erupt into open, armed conflict. Yet how could this happen? The Visible City had the arms, the resources, the technology. In the usual terms—logistics, strategy, fire-power—it could achieve victory within hours. The Invisible City, considering its traditions, the very premise of its existence, might not even call for resistance.

I refer now to reports of a secret meeting in the Visible City of the responsible military and civil leaders. If my sources are correct, the possibility of an attack was discussed but quickly rejected. This on the grounds that the basic documents upon which it was founded expressly forbid such action. Especially telling were the phrase "We, the People" and the accompanying words "One nation under God.". . .

2.

A few days later, two proposals were offered. One was for a public referendum, with a ballot that listed a series of alternatives: toward unity or toward an ordered, defined separation. The other was for an appeal to the Circle of Judges who had jurisdiction, at least nominally, over both Cities. Finally it was decided to combine both the appeal and the referendum. (The vote alone could be construed as merely an expression of public opinion.)

3.

And this is how it stands today: the Circle of Judges has agreed to hear the case. Depositions are being taken, briefs prepared, the whole machinery has been set in motion. One positive result is that there is less fear, less talk about armed conflict . . . . Later news indicates, however, it may well be years before a decision is reached. One reason for the delay, it appears, is that public pressure is being exerted on the Judges to disclose their places of resi-

dence. According to polls released a few days ago, a majority be-
lieve this would affect their decision . . . . One of the Judges has
just decided to disqualify himself. The thought that others
might follow his example has given rise to further uneasiness—
and as of this writing, we remain suspended between impossible
alternatives.

1980/1981

More than a Thing

for David Gascoyne

1.

There was not enough to describe, to record. There was just the moment when, responding to her call, he entered and saw the spidery *thing* scoot across the pillow. He remembered making some kind of motion, then hearing her say: *It has as much right to be here as we have.* Was that in response to his gesture, or a message to herself? He had said something, then returned to the other room; standing beside the window, the sky and water claimed his attention....

2.

They were in the house beside the sea. It was after a day spent walking on the beach, watching the boats move past the stone jetty . . . . They had returned in late afternoon. The wind had come up—not cold enough for a fire, but making it right for a drink, for the tape playing Vivaldi....

3.

What after all was this "it"? Was his gesture, seen through her eyes, one that invited defense of the fragile *thing?* To make it more real, he could summon the image, even make a drawing, but that would be using the lines, the paper itself, as a substitute reality...

4.

... Something moved beyond the window. It was a doe standing there head raised, neck arched, immobile. He was ready to turn, to call the woman, when a second doe appeared. He wondered then: Who are the witnesses, the intruders? Again, the slightest gesture could be interpreted as a threat. Yet if he remained silent, they might miss the unique moment, the moment come alive with their sharing....

1981

Chance Scripts
Selected Prose Poems
1970–1987

The Concert Hall / The Big Tent / The Pasture

"Music is intermittent . . . the continuity is in the listening."
—Thoreau

1.

Consider this a farewell to you, my audience. Sending you this message, I set aside the musical skills I have developed slowly, painfully over the years. Some of you may regard this use of words, instead of music, as a sad mistake. That you will have to determine for yourselves. I know, however, that if I had attempted to reach you in the cloistered, enclosed space of the concert hall, it would have been perceived as an intrusion, a violation. Imagine the scene: the orchestra has just concluded its tuning up; there are a few moments of awkward silence; the heavy, dark curtain parts; and I, the composer, step forth and begin what—incredibly—sounds like a lecture . . . .

2.

. . . I am standing in an open field preaching to the cows. The cows, the trees, the grass, the birds are too busy with the light, the wind, to be even called indifferent . . . . Nothing good, you say, can come of this. It is time to leave the scene, to exit in a graceful, dignified silence. Well, you are probably right—at least in the rational, logical world. I ask though: what alternatives are there? My friends have by now all taken their places inside either the Concert Hall or the Big Tent. When I was younger, I did briefly appear in the Big Tent. The gaiety, the exuberance was appealing. But I soon learned I had none of the temperament, the personality of the performer. Now only the performers are in demand, and to follow their example, I would have to follow in their footsteps . . . .

3.

And to follow their example, I would have to follow in their footsteps . . . . The words repeat, this time with a different sound. As I hear it now, this would mean to exchange the sense of failure with an equally ambiguous, equally depressing notion of success. For what do the success seekers bring to their chosen art, and what do they take away? Whatever it is or was, something is lost in the process. What poured forth as original, undeniable impulse is now arranged to meet an established taste or longing. After a while, there is something even the most accomplished virtuoso, playing the prescribed music, can no longer call forth. If you have guessed that this has happened to me, you are probably right. You may then be more sympathetic to my decision to move off-stage and take my place, unobtrusively, among you in the audience....

4.

... What is to come of this, this period of prolonged listening? I cannot as yet be sure of what I hear, but strangely there is a greater clarity in what I see. I hope I will not be ridiculed for this, but at the moment what I perceive is a "thread" of sound. But where the thread might be leading, I cannot tell. So far it just seems to go on unwinding, drifting through the air .... Is the end result of all this intense listening to be nothing more than what the ancients already knew? *Not the play or the players—but the played upon?* For was it not the word itself, the word as music, of which the Psalmist sang: "I will incline mine ear to a parable: I will open my dark saying upon the harp." *Upon the harp,* I hear myself echoing, *upon the wind.*

1981/1986

Goodbye to a Village

1.

I had thought to remain here, without interference, as long as I wanted to. But the arrival of the letter—with its vague suggestion I might be needed elsewhere—has put this into question. While telling myself not to be upset, I have begun a kind of reprise, to consider not only what brought me here but what has kept me here . . . . Going back to first impressions: the view of winding streets, red-tiled roofs, the village itself surrounded by small, friendly hills. For once I felt I had arrived where there was no split between being and belonging. Almost from the start, I noticed a quick, easy acceptance by those who were born and would die here . . . .

2.

My stay here may indeed be drawing to a close. I should have known this even without the letter. Signs of this now whenever I appear on the street. Where before there were special greetings, now there is a slight, embarrassed smile, a quick departure. I connect this somehow with the recent arrival of a small group—with whom I share the same language—whose presence has yet to be defined. It has even occurred to me that they may remain, as replacements, after I have gone. I have noticed already that their presence has brought something alien to the spirit of the village. So far there is no direct evidence, but I have begun to look at their faces, listen to their voices, with ever closer scrutiny . . . .

3.

A sudden disturbing thought: Couldn't the same suspicion have greeted me on my arrival? For who knows what brings one to these remote places and how one is perceived by the inhabitants? It is hard to tell, even for oneself, whether one is in search of or in flight from something. All the visible signs, and my own feeling, suggested I had come to the right place. But I was especially careful to avoid any self-deception. After all, I was among people for whom betrayal was almost a daily occurrence. I realized I would have to earn their trust, not seek their gratitude . . . . How different it seems for the recent arrivals! Already there are expressions of discontent, of having come here too late, or to the wrong place . . . .

4.

Does it make any difference whether I stay or go? The inhabitants continue with their lives, performing their simple tasks, as they always have. Still I find it hard to avoid the question: *But for how much longer?* As for the recent arrivals, what is this village to them? Perhaps no more than just another part of their floating world, to be talked about, written about, and then abandoned. One can almost predict the course of their disenchantment, followed by the withdrawal, the whispers: *Not here: This is not the place.*

5.

I realize now I should be grateful for the opportunity presented by the letter. For the chance to leave before the rumors start that there is another village—closer to the forest, the jungle—where the "real people" may be found. My mind turns toward what stirred me so deeply when I arrived. The women in the marketplace, kneeling among the shawls and pottery, or offering for sale those incredible blue- and orange-colored mushrooms. The woodcutters at first light, setting off for the tree-lined hills, the donkeys alongside, their lifelong companions. The small boys carrying strapped to their backs unknown burdens, whatever anyone paid them to carry . . . .

6.

And what to say to these burdened children? I could tell them about the letter: "They wrote to me and said it was time . . . ." But what would that sound like to those who have never been taught to read? They would have to imagine a voice that comes from elsewhere and gives orders that are to be followed. But these are the children who are born and die here, without ever having known any *elsewhere!*

And is there anything to tell the recent arrivals? I could try saying, *Mira, no más.* Just look, that's all. But that, I suppose, is what they cannot do. For even the sight of those faces, those ancient time-haunted eyes, and their illusions, their personal quests and adventures, might come to an abrupt and intolerable end.

1970/1986

Limbo

Once more I have written a book. With what in mind and at what effort, I do not intend to say. I acknowledge though that I have thought and rethought, written and rewritten, calling upon all I know and can imagine. And the result is—something the world has surely the greatest need of—another book. But even as I write this, I recognize the poor attempt at humor. For it is not "another," it is this book—or even, so help me, *the book*.

What is still difficult to admit, now that it is out there, is that it is now in the hands of *strangers*. But that may give the wrong impression, for it has not yet found a publisher. And as things stand, it may never be published. What then do I mean by saying it is "out there"? It seems obvious: out of my hands and into "theirs."

. . . I see now what I have retreated from, what I have avoided saying. It means what it has always meant, though unacknowledged, unstated: it is *I* who have been placed in the hands of strangers. And the terrible thing is that I alone have made this choice, have sought this result, have persisted through endless hours, painful choices, all in order to . . .

1981/1986

The Book / The Mailing

... At last the day comes when I appear, nervous but in good spirits, at the bookbinder's. As he hands me the wrapped parcel, he advises me not to look inside, but to take it at once to the post office. Time was when I could not have done this, could not have trusted myself that much. But now I feel more in charge, prepared to handle the doubts, the longing for just one more look.

... Very well, then: the book is not only written, but printed and bound. After the long struggle with words, sentences, chapters, I can begin to live again as others live. No detours, I tell myself, straight to the post office . . . . Arriving there I go to the nearest window. Standing behind it is an attractive young woman in a dark blue cotton smock. As she asks the contents, I tell her it is a book. Of course, she says, and you must be the author. When I nod agreement, she is pleased, excited. She calls over a few of her coworkers. *Good luck,* they say, *all the best for you and your book. . . .* I leave in the best of moods. I have done what I set out to do. I am wise enough now to know that the story is like all other stories: someone is falling in love, someone is dying, someone is being born. . . .

... Does it matter that the book was lost in transit? That someone planted a bomb in the mailbox, and all that was left was a few charred fragments? Some of you may think that was a terrible outcome. But you would be wrong. For the fact is, as we both know, it was lost the moment it left the hands of the author . . . .

1970/1986

The Error Catastrophe

... F.'s return is unexpected. He phones one morning, having just arrived from the East Coast. In spite of my resolve not to permit any more unscheduled visits, I agree to see him .... A half hour later, he is at the door. Not much change since his last visit, about two years ago. He is still shy, almost inarticulate, except on the subject of his work. But since he is the only scientist I've known for a long period of time, I still find this interesting. (As much of it, at least, as I can understand.) His news is that he has been working on some compounds that may have an analog in nature. I sense his excitement, even though these exist at present only in the laboratory. He is confident, in his quiet way, that his results will be verified, duplicated. (Later in the day, after his departure, it occurs to me that his compounds are, and may remain, genuine enigmas. Reflecting further, I attempt an aphorism: *The incomparable is also the impenetrable.*)

*

... I have been trying, in exchange, to tell him something of what I'm working on. For it seems necessary to preserve the semblance of a dialogue, even though our words may falter at the edge of contrasting worlds. My writing too, I say, seeks some kind of analog in nature. Feeling somewhat reckless, I venture that there is a metaphor that makes relations apparent, but also metaphor as analog that transcends scale. Something in these words (I'm not sure what) suggests what he calls "the error catastrophe." It sounds very strange—as though nature has calculated in advance how to profit from its own mistakes. Those scientists, he says, who subscribe to this view even call themselves "catastrophists." I get the strange feeling that confirmation of this belief among them would be important, no matter what it includes.

*

100

. . . Our words move back and forth from one world to another. Through it all, the word *analog* serves as a bridge, a point of reference. As I keep trying to translate his experience into familiar terms, I suddenly remember Rene Daumal's book, *Mount Analog*. I tell him briefly about the quest, about the travelers climbing a symbolic mountain. His response startles me: "I'll be leaving here in the morning. Going to do some hiking." And he names a nearby mountain. In a sense that finishes the conversation, for although I repeat the name of the book, I'm sure he will never read it. . . .

*

. . . I keep trying, after he leaves, to remember more of what the book contains. And trying to connect it with his pursuit of those peculiar compounds. (Which presumably have been there all along, waiting to be discovered and named.) I feel somewhat resentful, as if I had failed to say what most needed saying: that his empirical search is just as saturated with illusion as anything encountered by Daumal's nebulous group of travelers on their own basically unbelievable mountain.

1981/1986

The Candidate / The Canceled Child

1.

Let it be known: no matter what the inducements, I am not a candidate. Those who are—their names are known to you—have worked hard and long to get their names in lights, their faces on the screen. And by offering their faces, their names for public inspection, they may fill a need, provide some essential service. I don't happen to believe this, but on rare occasions it might be the case....

2.

What brings this to mind is a recent conversation with an editor of a small, new publishing firm. We were meeting for the first time, talking generally about writers whom we both knew. I noticed a large manuscript displayed prominently on his desk. As he followed my glance, he reached over and handed it to me. When I indicated that the name was unfamiliar, he said it was the work of a talented young poet who had suicided a month before at the age of twenty-five. I thought at first that some real question was involved—something for me to understand or comment on—but as I handed it back, he said, "This is going to be a valuable property."

3.

What did I start to say? Something about personal politics in the literary scene, and the curious resemblance—as the microcosm to the macrocosm—it has to politics on the grand scale. At least that's what I had in mind. Yes, I know now: the Candidates—the self-advancers—were to be the target. But surely that is too obvious for comment. More important is what happened to G., dead at twenty-five: *canceled.* For if we are to really consider this, we may find the prototype within a long tradition.

There is something to be said for the intensity of the short life. And there is some peculiar connection with the intensity that the Candidate seeks and generates. As if there might be some failed or dead artist buried deep within them. Next time you find yourself standing close to one of them, try looking closely, notice what is missing from his eyes . . . .

1981/1986

Framis: More or Less Himself

1.

Those who have heard of him—one time or another, one country or another—will have doubts about what follows. They may call this a biased, personal report, and frankly so it is. I start with a statement you may accept or reject: Framis can appear anywhere, anytime. Need I add: in one of his many aspects? It is not merely a question of disguise or costume, but that his *being* and his *seeming* are in fact inseparable. This I have come to believe is his greatest strength, the source of his most lasting appeal. For he does not, as those we see every day, derive from a cluster of fictions. It would be more correct to describe him as a natural force, a kind of weather.... I might go on in this vein, using various metaphors, making all sorts of claims. But this would only underline my belief that Framis cannot be contained or defined within the usual boundaries....

2.

Framis was, Framis is, Framis will be. I say this as quietly, as gently as the words permit. Others of course might not be so circumspect. In the present climate, with its ambiguous longing for both the exalted and the debased, one can imagine Framis as Saint, as Sinner, within a scenario that places him one moment in the public eye, the next in some elusive, subterranean existence. Some kind of cosmic traveler, moving not merely across the earth, but in some grander, wider space. So that wherever he goes, whenever he returns, he stretches our tolerance for the incredible....

3.

... I have been asked once more to confirm the rumors of Framis's impending return. I can only say that, sooner or later, in one form or another, he will reappear. Whether this will satisfy our most urgent need, that is another matter. For it is possible that instead of rejoicing, we may feel let down or angry. We may witness, then, what we are not prepared to accept or approve. I have in mind certain occasions when he transformed a whole array of props, which he first summoned, then made disappear. As I recall, these included a large tub of wet cement, a dangling rope, a plaster tree—along with various other insidious and anxious objects. There are those who, on the basis of this, predict that, in his next "materialization," he may feel inclined to do away with such items as a dressmaker's dummy, an enormous pincushion, a fur-lined teacup. Items which have for so long dominated the symbolic landscape of our time.

4.

And now to conclude, I offer a few key words essential to understanding what Framis is really about: *dream* and *redeem, resist* and *exist.* Words I have heard him say not once but many times. But one must not be surprised if he follows these serious, almost programmatic words with some incredible gesture. Like pulling a hair from his beard and handing it to you: "Here, use this for a filament." And be ready if, a moment later, his physical being begins to contract—growing smaller and smaller until there is nothing, absolutely nothing, left but an aura, a charged space . . .

1982/1985

The Lost Parable

"We show ourselves at our best, or worst, in how we feel about what we have lost."

—R. W. Wainwright

1.

It is no longer possible to think of the text as misplaced or missing. Too much time has passed for that. I have to admit the loss and, as so often before, put it out of mind. And yet, and yet . . . Mind has so many recesses and residues, who can tell what may yet slip through in an unexpected, unguarded moment? And even if it is beyond any literal retrieval, it may still find some other existence. I mean, aside from the physical text, that it may be constellated in one mind or another, where its "home" is memory . . . . This is no vain hope, for there are indeed those whose memory can be called upon. As it happens, I asked one recently if she remembered that afternoon—about a year ago—when I had read the parable to a group of mutual friends. She answered, "But of course: it was at Bill's house. You read the one about the forest." She supplied a few references that coincided, rather closely, with my own memory. Then she added, to my surprise, that she had talked with a few of the others, and they had agreed it was one of my best pieces of writing.

2.

It is this, I now realize, that I find so depressing. It is hard to deal with the thought that I have been unable to equal these lost words. But what I have written since has lacked some quality I find hard to define. I cannot make the comparison, for all I remember is a small part of the content: A small group of adult students has signed up for a tour of an area designated as wilderness. The "tour" has included lectures and seminars on survival: the search for edible plants, construction of emergency shelters, what to do upon losing a sense of direction, how to deal with predatory animals, etc. All this I can recognize as proposed by the rational, conscious mind. What was strange (how did I come

to write this?) was a group activity called *Hunt the Abandoned Child.*
This was not merely a game but a climax of the survival tests. I re-
call also that there was available, for those who remained for the
whole course, several units of school credit. But of course this
was optional....

3.

Why does it sound so like a dream? Yet I remember having
worked hard and long on the writing. In any case, there was the
reading before the group. The comments, I recall, were cer-
tainly favorable, if less than ecstatic. It is only now that I hear this
unqualified praise.... This should be enough, I realize, to make
me suspicious. But I have to stop thinking entirely about these
missing pages and show, instead, the confidence and strength of
mind to move past this latest disappointment. As with all that is
gone and "forgotten," there will be compensation in having con-
ceived the work, given it existence. As for what may happen
now, there is an impetus, a residue that lives on. I believe what I
have to believe: that it will make its presence felt—perhaps just
at that moment when I face the blank page that waits to be
inscribed....

1981/1986

Second to the Wolf

... He heads north until he reaches a place with a name: Glacier Bay. That is, it has a name, is marked on his map. Beyond that there is nothing: no dwellings, no inhabitants. But this is where he has planned to pitch his tent. It is still daylight, late afternoon. As he unpacks his gear, prepares to build a fire, a wolf appears.... Listening to him tell this, we sense his excitement. The year before, we recall, it was sighting an eagle that climaxed the trip. In other years (each year at this time he heads north, to the same general area) there was an encounter with a bear. Another time he came upon an old Indian camp which apparently no one before him had come across .... We begin to wonder: Why the wolf? The story, in fact, has no climax: just the wolf standing there, for a long time, watching him, then taking off through the woods .... He has presented it, though, as a culmination of past experiences. Which only begins to make sense when he tells us this was his last trip. He says that it ended *perfectly:* at last the one thing that was missing .... His joy and our resentment. We who have never even dreamed of this kind of adventure. Who have always required the known in the known circumstance: the house, the street, the city, the voice that speaks directly to us .... Now his voice changes from exultation to something vague, uncertain, as he says: *No more* .... *can't keep it up* .... The conversation ends with his saying he'll see us next year. The promise has the sound of resignation: going *south,* where we live, is evidently a poor alternative. It is clear then, in spite of the long friendship, what we really are to him: *second to the wolf.*

1981/1986

108

No Time for Gestures

"When we die, we don't leave the world—rather it leaves us. "
—Edvard Munch

It has happened so often that the idea is ingrained. Our journeys have been of limited duration, to a known destination. And each departure has been followed by a return. At some point, however, we start to think about, even prepare for, a departure that is without return. It is then that we find ourselves—like actors learning a new part—rehearsing certain gestures. We wonder then: which is the most appealing, the most appropriate? Lacking an audience and not trusting the verdict of the mirrors, we cannot tell which to choose. We continue setting the scene, summoning various colors and textures, trying to decide about music and speech, makeup and costume . . . . Someone is sure to ask at this point: does it have to be so theatrical? We do not respond but go on arranging the decor, the lights, the shadows. As if we could indeed enhance those last moments with an aura, a special intensity. But the rational mind, breaking in on this complicated reverie, tells us that *this* departure is not what we perform—but what is performed upon us.

*

All this could be written by anyone—with just an adequate imagination—in touch with their deepest fears and longings. What cannot be written, planned for, is what happens to come our way. As for instance this letter from a friend who quotes these words of Edvard Munch. Now it has come to my attention, I have still to think more and longer of what it means. If I read it right, there is no time for gestures. For it is not departure that we face, but an abrupt, unprecedented abandonment . . . .

1982/1986

A Picture in the Voice?

Where there is something to draw, there is something to draw upon. Are these words his own, or has he read them somewhere? Following the thought, he is not sure what it means. Perhaps that only what can be seen (perceived?) can be expressed. If nothing more is involved, it is too literal, too familiar. He is ready to let it go, turn his attention elsewhere. But there is a sudden feeling of uneasiness. As though what the mind has rescued from the void amounts only to this: no picture, no thing, no idea. So that the effort to put picture into words—or words into picture—is inherently a waste of time....

*

He stands in front of a mirror. What he sees reminds him only vaguely of what he used to see. For the aging face tells a different story. One that even now is being written on his flesh. He walks away, walks through the rooms that remind him of his life. On one wall is a photograph of his younger self; on another wall, from about the same period, is a pencil drawing, a portrait, done by a friend. Something to draw upon—*or something that defeats time and memory?* On other walls, pictures, various objects, masks, spread across where and what he has been. His presence, his being here, is linked with all this. The next step, he tells himself, is to decipher, to remember what all this means. But if this were possible, something else would be missing. *If only there was a voice in the picture—or a picture in the voice?*

*

At the threshold of nonsense and silence, he chooses silence.

1982/1986

The Feathers of My Wife

. . . Once more we are walking on the beach. As so often before, I see her hesitate, stop and search the sand. *What is it this time?* I see only sand—no pebbles, no shells, nothing. I walk on, certain she will follow in a moment. But then I too stop, turn and look back. She bends down, picks up a small gray feather. *A feather?* While I wait, she gathers a few more. There is about her an air of discovery, something in the way she holds them . . . . The sea calm; fishing boats anchored in the bay. One of the good days, I think, one of *our* better days. For a few moments she remains beside me, walking at the same pace. But she says nothing, her eyes continue probing the sand.

. . . I recall times we walked on other beaches, along this same coastline, or earlier, in other countries. Even then, I realize, we seldom walked side by side. Either I would lag behind, stopping to light my pipe, or she would be picking up this and that, accumulating her "treasures." I think of the crowded shelves at home: boxes crammed with pebbles, tinted glass, dried, brittle miniature crabs. . . .

*

The true distance, I think, is in the seeing. Our view of things, like our footsteps, never quite matched. The tinted glass, the shells, the pebbles—*and now the feathers?* What she saw in and through these things, I have yet to discover. For what I saw—what I see now—is the usual intersection of beach, sea, and sky. Children playing in the sand, seagulls diving, dogs running toward the water. What is there to add; what is there to take away? What has escaped me, what has escaped her, that this is not enough?

1983/1986

Between Worlds

An interview with M. in the morning paper. Now seventy, he has just published his twentieth book, a memoir of his early years. The photograph shows him much the same as when I last saw him, ten or twelve years ago. I remember how I kept urging friends to read him as one of the most neglected of our novelists. How remote it seems now, thinking of all those "vanished worlds." Still I am touched by M.'s reference to "memory and emotion" as essential to the imagination. This while one wonders if there are any serious readers left. . . .

A letter just received from a young writer. He insists on the need for "new vantage points." He says there must be alternatives to the established forms: different words for a different time. I place the letter beside the interview. The two voices resonate a dilemma. I wonder if these split allegiances are inevitable, or can somehow be reconciled. . . .

All this has had more impact than I expected. I have been trying now to write things that reflect these different ways of seeing. The result is confusion, close to chaos. For if M.'s "memory and emotion" is set aside, what is left may be mere information, mechanical noise. While the other view, which seeks surprise, discovery, may achieve only the brief span of novelty. . . . It has occurred to me, in the last few days, there is within us—beyond the level of "citizen," of "artist"—two distinct creatures. One sets off to join the thirsty herd, in search of nourishment at the waterhole. The other, with the same features and form, moves slowly, inexorably in the direction of the darkening hills. . . .

1981/1986

112

The Agony of Crevices

For those who have not heard the sound—imagine twilight in one of those bleak, shattered places—I assure you it can be both painful and puzzling. There is a sense of vanished worlds, brought closer as one thinks of the ravaged, the unavenged, the homeless dead . . . . A few days ago I was reading the report of an obscure archaeologist, written early in the century. What struck me was a brief reference to "a peculiar *humming noise,* apparently issuing forth from between the stones." Still trying to absorb this, I read further: "Strange to be hearing this—since it was on the evening of the very day we had decided to abandon the site."

*

The space between? Cries and whispers of the abandoned—heard just when their story was about to be told? It seems quite fanciful, yet I wonder: We know about those vast trenches where victims of plague, war, genocide, are buried, but what of those small fissures between earth and stone? Who knows what worlds of betrayal, of chilling, dreadful secrets might be hidden there? So far this is beyond the range of even our most advanced, most delicate instruments. But some day we may hear and be able to decipher the message. And trace that *humming noise* back to those torn from life, voicing in strange syllables their abandonment and neglect. Then we will know what is concealed within the agony of crevices. The question then will be: how to respond to their fractured voices, in chorus with the impatient cry of the as yet unborn?

1978/1986

One Vote for the Vulture

... He had written of the growing feeling of menace in the city, the alternative of moving to the country. But had added a kind of symbolic warning: "Those who consider this, however, should know that the vulture, the dreadful image, is sometimes mistaken for the hawk, the symbol of freedom."

But reading this, she found it hard to accept. The hawk, she said, had nothing to do with freedom. Witness the fieldmouse plucked from the grass, the tiny cries unheard by an indifferent, amoral sky. On the other hand, she thought that one might respect, if not admire, the essential role of the vulture: "Without him the landscape would be littered with half-digested, torn-apart creatures...."

*

It comes to mind for both of them while walking on the beach, at the sight of the torn body of a baby seal. They stand for a moment, looking up at the birds circling, looking down at the flies on the wet, gray flesh. Ahead of them is a stone jetty marking the end of the beach. They set off in that direction, slowly and in silence. They watch a few fishing boats heading out toward the open sea . ... He looks up, scanning the clear sky; the vultures are now out of sight. He extends his hand; their fingers close. For a while they walk this way; then as they turn toward home, their fingers loosen. They move further and further apart....

1981/1986

114

A Stone Taking Notes

"Somewhere among us a stone is taking notes. "
—Charles Simic

1.

Surely not your ordinary stone: something that appears in the field of vision, that you glance at and turn away from. The poet calls it "a stone," but bestows upon it a special, unique status. What goes through the mind, if we decide to honor the poet's imagination, may be something like this: can a mere stone be so endowed, transformed, elevated? Doesn't this usurp the role of listener: our role? And note that the poet doesn't stop there: he implies that the stone is positioned somewhere out of sight. *Somewhere?* The location is left vague enough to suggest a disturbing mystery. For while the next words—*among us*—apparently shorten the distance, it remains remote and hidden. As for the concluding words—*taking notes*—surely this augments our uneasiness, plays upon the surface of our always latent paranoia . . .

2.

Assume this is indeed a stone set apart from all others, from any we have noticed or studied. Try then to visualize color, shape, size—even adding distinctive marks and scratches. Enough to make it identifiable. Does this mean we can convert *any* apparently anonymous object into an efficient "machine"—or even a piece of art? A thought I find both intriguing and depressing. For it opens the possibility that the designated object may have or acquire personality, judgment, will—even desire. (A stone's "desire" is a subject we may speculate upon freely—for who could prove us wrong?) And since we have gone this far, say that a stone's most profound, most secret desire is to discard its anonymity, to be emblemized: *Rosetta, Sphinx, Pyramid, Cleopatra's Needle,* etc. We may add to this list others that, for one reason or another, have achieved their own eternal name.

3.

At this point someone *among us* (!) is sure to claim we are better off without emblems. But someone else, more experienced, wiser, is likely to reply: Without emblems there can be no legends. Without legends, we can have no heroes. Without heroes, all that is menacing, inaccessible must remain that way . . . . Out of reach those distant icefields and moonfields, never to know the sound of live footsteps and answering voices . . . . But then suddenly it occurs to us: if a stone can take notes, why not also record, store, transmit? Imagine retrieving the sound of vanished worlds: dinosaurs mating, the great cry of perishing populations before the flood, the fire, the erupting volcano . . . . A stone that survives, tells this much, yet leaves some part of its secret coded message intact, some faint signal, not quite decipherable, that might signify another chance, another dawn for consciousness.

1982/1986

How Tall Was Toulouse-Lautrec?

The film presents the life. Costume and decor, choreography and spectacle offer entertainment as evidence. The paintings, the posters dissolve; what remains is a vague memory of a few staged scenes. One is of the actor, absurdly dressed in black and white formal clothes. We see him bowing, tipping the stovepipe hat. But this only reminds us: it is the *actor*, not the artist, who claims our sympathy, touches our sense of pathos and distress. . . . Another scene: interview with his mother in the elegant, high-ceilinged room. Closeup of the mother's face: the absence of any real suffering. A dialogue between strangers. Sense of tradition and privilege enforcing a politeness—a conspiracy to pretend—that obscures everything.

*

Toulouse-Lautrec in the café with the cancan dancers. The faces, the figures remind us of what—somewhere else—is real art. The posters come to mind at the same moment that they appear on the screen. They appear now, in closeup, faded and peeling from the wall, in the relentless rain . . . . The scene shifts to the warm, dry rooms of the whorehouse, where he relaxes in the profusion of ample, perfumed flesh. Here he is known and welcome, in this refuge from loneliness and isolation. The women carry on a bantering conversation, while he sits propped, doll-like, on the edge of the bed . . . . *How tall was Toulouse-Lautrec?* The absurd question enters the mind from some unlikely source. *Tall, dark and handsome.* What brings the cliché, the stereotype? Something in us that equates endurance and pain with the romantic hero. In any case, the absurd image drives out the real biography of the real man. But in a few minutes, the counterimage returns: the bulging back, the too-large head, the withered legs. Not a freak in this version, but a creature at home in a world he has created for himself. *At home?* We are more inclined to place him—the man, not the actor—among those on whom life has played its cruel joke. Is there a kinship with all of those, or some of those? Is there for him, *for them,* some "compensation" that might sustain the soul—beyond neglect and ridicule?

*

About that kinship: imagine the spirit of the dead artist entering a procession of the freaks and dispossessed. Think of them as having departed, bound for some other realm, not available to the more normal dead . . . . See them arriving in some undefined *elsewhere,* where their bruised and trampled souls may find refuge . . . . Imagination will not take us all the way, but permits us to approach the threshold, the boundary. From there, night after night, we may hear sounds of music, of rejoicing. Enough to suggest that Giant and Dwarf have found not only solace, but at last fulfillment of their dearest, wildest dreams.

1981/1986

Among Other Things

"The freedom of each word, punctuated by an obscurity."
—Andre Du Bouchet

1.

Silence prints upon the page. Black letters assemble into a pattern; one by one the words, the sentences form. We follow across and down the page; we enter into and depart from a series of realities. We observe here turning into there, then into now, there and then into elsewhere. All at once a particular place and time emerges, seeks its specific image, its undeniable name. Event follows event, encounter follows encounter. From all this, something we have come to think of as "the real subject" has begun to emerge....

2.

I have written your name and placed it somewhere. More precious when the scrap of paper is apparently lost and then by accident found again.... Holding it in my hand, I notice that the letters are small, the handwriting almost indecipherable. What is missing, of course, is your face, your voice.... As I recall it now, I saw your face, that first time, without hearing your voice. You were standing on a red-tiled floor in a small alcove beside a row of white candles. I watched from a distance as you leaned forward and blew them out one by one. It was too soon to come forward, to announce myself. It occurred to me then: for every being born, endowed with a name, there is another who remains unsignified, at home in the dark.

3.

So at times the lost one is retrieved, identified. The dialogue that began so suddenly—and stopped without apparent reason—begins again. Begins where it left off: with your passionate references to the living beast. The beast, you said, may be perceived in different ways. As the target, to be approached with our sharpest, deadliest weapons. But also as the object of worship, to be garlanded with flowers, paraded in ritual procession . . . . I believe you went on like this for some time. Finally I had heard enough. What has all this, I asked, to do with men, with the rulers of men? We both know that the statue may be toppled, the monument destroyed by the raging crowd. The King may be deposed, exiled to a bleak, distant island . . . .

4.

Suppose then that we arranged to meet on that same island. Suppose even that we were to send word to the King that we would like to be invited for lunch or for tea. Awaiting his response, we could spend time on the beach. We could talk of this and that, pretend that we understand each other. Whether the invitation comes or not, we could agree to meet again—perhaps the following year. We could even send word to our closest friends: come and join us where the sky is lettered, where the late glow is Byzantine.

5.

. . . Already you have begun drifting off, returning to the wind and fog of memory. Are you going then—once more to assume your true reality in the realm of *back there and then*? It brings to mind one of your previous incarnations and disappearances. The last words you said were "If only the world was a brighter place." I watched you then turn silently toward the shadows on the wall. And I thought: if only we could go back to that morning in the Cathedral, when we followed the monks in their trailing robes . . . . Dear friend, don't you see that even now, at the very moment of your departure, there is some other vague figure coming toward us. Notice the grave courtesy of his silent, almost imperceptible, greeting. And if either of us were to ask him "Will it be any different next time we meet?"—surely we both know the answer.

1973/1986

Question of a Shovel:
Notes Toward—and Away From—the Writing of a Poem

"Deeper than the summer
The shovel breaks,
Deeper than the cry
In another dream "

—Yves Bonnefoy[*]

"There is no way to read about people who lived
a million years ago. We must find their bones. "

—Kamoya Kimeu[†]

"Deeper in our lives, in our minds
Than any song, than any pictures "

—George Oppen [‡]

1.

Two items in the morning paper, juxtaposed, bring forth the thought, present a challenge. The first is of an unnamed city official reacting to new rumors of a long-delayed building project: "I'll believe it when I see the shovel." The second is the story of Kamoya Kimeu, the fossil-hunter, the man from Kenya. Turning from one to the other, I sense opposing views of reality. The city official seems to be saying: *Wait for the tangible reality; the rest is conversation.* While the fossil-hunter, already renowned for his discoveries, reminds us of what takes place in the mind as one reaches the source . . . . *Whatever comes to mind, comes to eye, comes to hand.* I have written this somewhere, and wonder now if it is true. I summon the image of the clenched hands, the weathered wood, the stained blade. With a little further effort, I picture the body twisting, the blade thrust toward the ground . . . . I recall the recent digging in the vacant lot across the street. The scene shifts to another place, another time: a desert in Africa, a mountain in Brazil . . . . I sense the questions forming—questions I do not feel prepared to answer. A number of literary allusions come to mind; none are adequate to the real act in a real landscape. Not words, but experience, must tell the tale. And I have held and used a shovel so seldom that . . .

2.

. . . Shovel lying flat on the ground. Who left it there, for what reason? It belongs in the potting shed, with the other tools, found there when we moved into the house. Strange that, in all these years, I have never questioned their presence. I assumed they were left there by the former owner for work in the garden . . . . *There was that other garden, where we entered going past the iron gates: tropical flowers, the perfumed air in a secluded place above the drowned city . . . . That other garden, the high-walled garden where the children were playing. Gunfire in the distance. The children led away, never to return . . . .*

3.

The mind moves abruptly from *garden* to *trench*. And not just a small, shallow trench, but something wider, deeper that extends somewhere out of sight. Something to stand up in or crouch down inside while exploding objects fall from the sky . . . . So after all these years, I have come to the question of the shovel. To wonder how this simple tool has retained its integrity, its basic shape through all the wars, the disasters, the tedious, painful attempts to rebuild, to restore . . . . What occurs to me is that the shovel is in the shoveling (as the hammer is in the hammering). The unexpected words restate the question: Who is shoveling and for what reason? Shovels raised and lowered. Shovels digging a trench, a tunnel—but also sifting through debris, through mounds of garbage . . . . *What can be retrieved, what can be redeemed?* Something forms at the edge of perception. It may be a dream, a film, a memory. Suddenly there is a city, many cities; at their outer limits, in the early morning light, crowds gather. Bent bodies cluster around piles of rubbish; busy hands scrounge and forage for something to use, to repair, to sell. For a chair, a table, a blanket, a child's toy—whatever can be carried off to the squatter's shack, the tarpaper shelter . . . .

4.

But it is too hard to dwell on this. The mind seeks alleviation: something more tolerable, more pleasant. I look beyond the cities, beyond the hills, to the shore of a calm, blue sea. Inevitably, as I sift through the familiar images, there is a child playing in the sand. As remembered, almost as ordered, he holds a toy shovel, moves dirt into and out of a toy pail. After a while, he throws the shovel aside, begins scooping and shaping the moist sand. He has something in mind—whatever it is, it confirms an element in the child's world, bringing a smile of recognition and pleasure ... Perhaps it is not too different from those who are digging for shards and artifacts, when they find fragments that connect a missing part of their world. Among them I place now the man whose picture is in the morning paper: the fossil-hunter, the man from Kenya: "There is no way to read about people who lived a million years ago. We must find their bones."

5.

And when we find their bones: will it tell us about ourselves as well? Will it be something we need to know, or prefer not to know? Will there be a small hole in the skull—made we guess by some vengeful instrument—a hole that narrows the distance between then and now? We have come this far with an image of a thing. But no single idea, no single image. For we have encountered along the way conflicting images: the shovel as toy, tool, weapon. For each one who thinks of uncovering new life, new growth, there are many who think only: it throws dirt on your face. We cannot choose among them, for none of them are wrong. We can only wonder at what sight or sound comes through our voices. Still unsure of what it is we have to tell, we feel a poem stirring, seeking a space not occupied by story and photograph ....

6.
Between shadow and stone
     between the hand that searches
     and the hand that is sought
let the shovel decide —
While Kamoya Kimeu having located the skull of a man
a million years old   probes now for the fingers —
Let the shovel decide   how far the blade goes in
between the delicate layers
     before the form emerges
that tells us what we were and are —
Let earth itself be witness
     to the mingled grass and blood
     as the red and green we live with
     the brown we have yet to imagine.

*Yves Bonnefoy, *Things Dying, Things Newborn,* translated by Anthony Rudolf, Menard Press, 1985.

†Steve Rubenstein, "Kamoya Kimeu: King of the Fossil-Hunters," *San Francisco Chronicle,* November 12, 1985.

‡ George Oppen, "Daybook," *Ironwood* 26, 1985.

Life & Death of a Guide

"Man's natural situation is to be disoriented and lost."
—Ortega y Gasset

"You can't get there from here."
—Irish proverb

Say that we are in fact here. That we have a legitimate desire, a sensible purpose in wanting to be there. It appears that we may begin to plan and prepare for departure. But as we look into the matter, we discover it is not that simple. For the "there" we have in mind appears in different places on different maps. A growing number of uncertainties stand in the way: besides the exact route, the availability of food and lodging, there is the unpredictable weather. All this combines to make us realize that its accurate name is *elsewhere*.

It is then that we are put to the test. Our need for and love of adventure is balanced against our instinct for self-preservation. And if these were the only alternatives, we might find ourselves stalemated, mired in a dilemma. But fortunately there is still the option of hiring a guide. Not the guide who only knows the trails in familiar places, but one who has himself survived passage through *terra incognita*.

I want to make it clear now that I am not recommending myself. I have been asked at different times to join a party of explorers—and once even to lead an expedition. I realized early that I had neither the temperament nor the stamina for such undertakings. I have on occasion, on request, offered a few words of "guidance," but that is all. Aside from this, especially in these latter years, I have not thought of going anywhere. I feel now that it is enough to be what one already is. Being here, then, has replaced the desire for going or getting somewhere. As for a voyage or journey to *elsewhere*, there is one that may require no effort or plan. Love is a companion that takes us to the boundary, but there is no guide across the threshold . . . . I begin to hear rumors that I can only identify as coming from the dead, the unborn. But it would be foolish, and premature, to repeat them.   1986

Say He Arrives There

Whether the image arrives or is somehow summoned, it is hard to tell. What appears though is the figure of a a man, hunched over, staring out across an immense, empty stadium. He is seated in a lower tier, somehow near the center; around him the deserted rows suggest an eerie, almost grotesque absence. Who is he? What brings him here? No clue in his appearance: an unlikely combination of introspection and anonymity. He could be a former athlete coming back for one more view of the playing fields, dreaming of past glories. Or a discharged employee—a grounds-keeper?—returning out of habit, having nowhere else to go. He could also be—are there any limits?—a confused sports fan, appearing on the wrong day, having forgotten to check the schedule. . . .

*

. . . As to what brings me here, I cannot be sure. There is an impulse to go where one is not expected, where one does not belong. One has had this feeling before, but this time it is stronger than any restraints: the desire to experience, in isolation, what attracts and motivates the passionate multitude. For what surrounds me here is the shared reality of witnesses to a contest that is part game, part war. This is what excites the crowd, allowing them to identify with those who perform the alternating roles of hero and victim. In this arena, physical encounters, given the status of events, are offered as the food of memory, the feast of legend.

. . . I feel impelled to rise now, to salute those enactments of triumph and disaster, those ghostly banners and emblems unfurled by the shifting wind. I turn and look above, below, all around me, wondering how to signify my presence.

And then I understand what I have to do: I bring my hands together in a slow rhythmic applause. A few moments later I feel ready to begin my speech . . . . It is hard to believe what I am hearing: a small but sympathetic response. It comes from one section, then another: voices sounding through their own silence, their own invisibility. I take my place with those who have yet to be heard, to be recognized.

1986

The Door to Have

Remember that she chose an austere landscape. That she lived in it and created—among other things—paintings of flowers. Nothing like the still lifes we had seen before, but the single flower, augmented, magnified. In pursuit of that vision—so we imagine—she placed next to the flower, a skull, a sky suffused with strong, clear light....

But we are getting away from *that door*, and what it might have signified. Assume then that it kept in what she needed to enclose; kept out confusion, distraction; helped her to focus what she faced day after day: sun, sand, stone. Shadows spreading as she returned to the focus of arrival and departure. Waiting for her—as she touched the hard, cool knob—was the threshold to inner space, refreshing as water in an earthen jar. The door she had to have: the precise marker in all that vast and void-like uncertainty....

But how could she have known that? Intuition we know can be correlative of will and desire, can offer its growing forms as deliberate as evidence. What is less obvious, harder to decipher, is how these forms flowered and danced in her mind. For something like this set in motion an intricate transaction between eye, mind, and hand—opened the way between paint and brush and canvas. The door, after all, did open and close; space within walls merged with space within herself....

... Walking past the paintings, we arrive at a world not seen before. Not sure yet what we are looking at, looking for. No single name, here or elsewhere, contains the whole array of thought and feeling. And yet there is the sense of something solid and self-sustaining. The knob itself is cool to the touch....

The Door to Have

Facing the desert on a copper morning
the sun factored her skin and mind:
imprint of the primary line waiting to find
its further life in paint—insistent questions
kept her returning to a dark still space
where whitewashed walls waited to be filled....

In retrospect we wonder how she survived
the light that swam through shadow: to create
the flower more predator than prey—something there
frightens even while it reassures: refraction
of will and desire upon the hard-edged door
closing upon the space that framed her eye and mind....

It was important to know she could step inside
and be there at the exact meridian to calculate
the orbit of earthly terrors: self-scaled delights—
Measure her mood and motive with the dry clear
transit of the desert night: guess how the fragrant stars
told her where landscape ended: where the worlds conjoined.

1986/1987

The Trouble with Keys

It was not that long ago that we read the story of the man waiting to be admitted by the Doorkeeper. The lesson of it was so powerful, so clear that it dominated our imagination. It was not that we were denied access, but our own passivity, our lack of self-esteem kept us outside . . . . How much has changed since then! One hardly ever hears now about the Door as an obstacle, a barrier. The Doorkeeper himself has, as it were, completely disappeared, forced perhaps to seek other employment, the occupation itself become anachronistic, obsolete. If we still have a problem with access, it is that with everything apparently available, we no longer know where to turn . . . .

I seem to have overstated the case. We still have a problem with access, but this appears now in a different light. It is no longer a problem with doors, but a problem with keys. I refer first to the common experience of misplacing and losing keys. Inquiry at various Lost and Found Departments reveals that of all the articles we deal with every day, it is the key that is lost most often . . . .

. . . Perhaps I cannot explain this after all. There is so much more to be considered than I realized. For one thing, it is not merely a matter of losing, but also of finding keys. This became clear to me the other day when, sorting through our collection, I found dozens of keys of various shapes and sizes that we had somehow accumulated. Some were rusty, tarnished, of different shapes than those now commonly used. Where were the doors to which they were originally fashioned? We thought of previous dwellings, here and in other houses, other cities, other countries. Even if a few might fit those doors that were part of our lifetime, our occupancy, there were others that belonged to another time, perhaps another century . . . .

. . . So we have come to this place and stand once more before the entrance. How can we tell what has brought us here, and if this is where we belong? *We have found the keys. But the doors are missing* . . . .

1986

Truth, War, and the Dream-Game

"God sees the truth, but waits."

—Tolstoy

There is something intriguing, but annoying, about this. Perhaps the sense of cosmic hesitation—even indifference. The closer we look, the more massive the ambiguity. The truth we know is so elusive, so *wayward* that it hardly deserves the name. Anything more is reserved for that rare state we call "revelation." (Approach this domain quietly, speak of it with a whisper.) As for the notion that the Source of revelation is Himself seeking revelation—isn't that wildly improbable?

What then is He waiting for? Our understanding is that truth, at this level, requires that perfect vision which is part of His very being—yet so remote from ours. To deny this, placing the mask of dream upon the face of truth, is illusion and madness. But our dream, our madness, is not ours alone. It is more of a dream within a dream, with the Ultimate Dreamer as the One who is also being dreamed....

All this is prelude to a recent dream of mine. Unfortunately the greater part disappeared shortly after I opened my eyes. What remains is this fragment: A group of men, seated at a long, narrow table, are waiting for God to make His presence known. Some are playing cards; some are studying large military maps spread out before them. I sense that these are not live figures, but spirits who have "passed over." I understand too that, in life, these were all top-ranking diplomats and generals.

After a while most of them move to one end of the table—leaving just a few cardplayers—and begin an animated discussion of various battles and campaigns of the Second World War. As they argue back and forth, it seems they are trying to work out a single, believable "story" to tell Him .... I find myself growing rather impatient, annoyed by His absence. Then suddenly it occurs to me: this meeting is taking place inside God's mind—*and nowhere else!* Yet the participants—used to power and command in their earthly existence—are performing as if nothing has changed.

131

They seem assured that, when He does arrive, it is their efficiency, not their guilt, which is to be considered. For surely He knows that they were only following orders....

As I tell it now, the dream seems more "political" than what I remember. For at the time of dreaming, what they said, or left unsaid, had lost its urgency. As if the war was only abstract, theoretical, and besides, too long ago, too far away. Their talk of troops, victories, defeats, logistics, almost an escape from boredom, a form of entertainment. What puzzled me more was the intensity and concentration of the cardplayers, who remained apart from all this....

Before this leaves the mind altogether, there is something else I need to remember. (I tell this with some reluctance but feel it has to be said.) More important, in some curious way, was the sense that the dead, when they reach their destination, bring along the same identity. That they retain some distinct features of what had been their individual consciousness. I found this so surprising, so *reassuring*, that I could put aside even the questions of collective guilt and divine irresponsibility.

As for the question I started with—*what then is He waiting for?*—that too appears in a different light. It seems now that it is *not* for the truth, which in any case He can perceive in an infinite number of ways. I feel it is more to the point to consider the "game playing" that centers around His presence or absence—even to ask if He needs to be taken seriously. It is as if He has located Himself inside a theatre of His own design and choosing. And what He is waiting for is for the curtain to come down. Whether this is for the end of the play, or for some next act, we cannot tell. If there is indeed a *next act*, will He offer us one that is better performed—or at least less threatening?

January 1987

The Place / The Name / The Child

"Get there if you can and see the land you once were proud to own."
—W. H. Auden

1.

Childhood: *another country*. She remembers the extraordinary size of an ordinary summer—the extended days dissolving into nights without number: a time without boundaries—and how suddenly it ended one morning with her mother's voice saying, "Time for school." All the strangeness of leaving the house— breaking one connection, as it were, before making another— and walking toward the school. The incredible distance that stretched out before her, block after block . . . . But when she returns as an adult, walks those few blocks—so ordinary and compact—she wonders: How could it be? The question brings other reminders of her changed size and status. There was the drawing she did one day in class: her parents seated at a round table, not looking at each other. On the back of the drawing—on an impulse—she had scribbled these words: "When we grow bigger, adults grow smaller."

2.

So we join other minds, in reverie, in the *community of memory*. Not in the search for what is lost, irretrievable, but to perceive, to validate, that earlier being. For the child, become *children*, surpasses the mode of specific circumstance. The question comes again: How could it be? Asking now what separates, or unites, one life and another. Asking also who it is that answers to a particular name, in a particular place and time. We sift through words and images: the sense of this, the color, the sound of that. Existence layers the real and mythical city. Main Street is interspersed with Byzantium and Bethlehem—we dwell there for a moment, with the thought of that luminous star.

3.

The voice that asks about this is joined now by a responding voice. Searching through dream and memory, the voices begin a dialogue of inner and outer worlds, of presence and absence . . .

—I wonder about that "luminous star." About the birth that takes place at the dying of the year. One can't help thinking of a child in winter: all those myths of renewal: the death that leads to resurrection . . . .

—What brings those myths into being? Perhaps that other view of winter: as a place, a time where snow covers everything. We glimpse a vague figure wandering through a vast, empty landscape. Appearance—and then disappearance—and that is all. There is no monument, no amulet, to discover or recover.

—No monument, no amulet, no name. Between monument and amulet, there is some difference of size and status. But the death of a child, or a king, makes no difference. The winds blow across sand and snow, across a timeless, spaceless space . . . .

—And for this we invent and imagine, making the myths more attractive and more complicated. But isn't this to obscure what we already know: that we implant, impose the name upon the place, merge one with the other, for the mind to make real? For the child that was to become *the person*: as having been, as going to be, remembered?

—To become the person is one thing: the one who is and is not. The one who does and is done to. Or as it appears in retrospect: the one who fails to do what has to be done.

—Perhaps that is how it appears on the scale of "me and my lifetime." But when we look across the river, toward the nearby mountain, our vision changes. For there all evidence of erosion and attrition is part of natural process. We arrive and depart, however, not as tree and stone, but under flexible schedules that we call "generations." What we add then, under the aegis of desire and longing, is that enlarged sense of being: THE CHILD AS ANCESTOR. The going to be again of what was: the beginning of dream without end . . . .

April 1987

Structural Pursuits
Prose Poems and Parables
1987–1990

The Photographers

1.

The photographers have come and gone. And with their departure, the house has begun to return to its familiar, comfortable state. Now once again, I tell myself, a wall is just a wall, a mirror just a mirror. No longer do I have to fend off the reflections of objects that somehow have acquired eyes—and not merely a placid gaze, but a kind of inquisitorial look. Yes, it is almost possible now to sit down somewhere, free of the sensation of being constantly under scrutiny. My situation here as tenant, as inhabitant, seems about to resume. For the shape, color, and form of things in their natural state, as themselves, has started to return....

2.

What am I trying to describe—or to avoid describing? It suddenly occurs to me that all this has the sound of a survivor: someone who wanders about the scene after a disaster. I understand this is an exaggeration. For in fact nothing has been broken, and by the usual standards, one could reasonably say "no harm done." More to the point, I realize now, is to ask what the photographers have done. The question is surely premature, since I have not yet seen the pictures. And perhaps there may be other, more pointed questions when they have become available. Of course this assumes that their promises will be kept, and the delivery made on schedule. But even if my suspicions are unfounded, and the photographs reach here after a reasonable interval, I would still wonder about the packaging, and whether they will have fulfilled their obligations as to size and quantity...

3.

...I have still not been able to face "the other, more pointed questions." I must do so now: Why did I agree to this in the first place? But even before that: How did they hear of me, and why was I selected? And why was it necessary to send four photographers—

137

all of them young and energetic—instead of one? Some of this I can answer: my name and address can be easily obtained. And when they called, they made it clear that I was one of several chosen, with the simple qualification expressed in the name of their project: *An Old Man in an Old House.* I went through a whole range of emotions when I heard this. And when I finally responded, it was hard to recognize the sound of my own voice: "Sure, why not?"

4.

... The pictures have finally arrived. They are indeed well packaged, and in the size and quantity specified. I cannot say that this is not what I expected, since I had no real idea what to expect. It is understandable, is it not, that I looked first for the portrait that would reveal this old man in this old house. Well, it turned out there was only one of me, seated at my desk. Aside from this there are several dozen posed arrangements of miscellaneous objects—mostly photographs of masks. And what is surprising, even startling, about this is that each of them—all four of these young enterprising photographers—has been photographed beside the masks, their own faces hidden, turned away from the light....

1989/1990

Words out of Reach

"It is easier to include the universe in a word than in a sentence."
—Marcel Havrenne

1.

. . . As for instance now, with the sense of something close, but just out of reach, that might bring a clearer, brighter view of things. This has come with the sudden awareness of a few words—as yet with no apparent connection—hovering as it were just at the edge of consciousness. *Place, name, remember.* After several efforts to combine them in a way that makes sense, I come up with this: "It was the name of a place one would have to remember." I recognize at once that this is far from satisfactory. I run through a series of variations, all equally ordinary, all leading nowhere . . . .

2.

. . . Still reluctant to let go, still getting nowhere. All I can do now is open the mind to other possibilities—whether they relate to this or not. What is going on here? I can't seem to distinguish between articulation and communication. If I were only trying to articulate, I believe I could sooner or later find the appropriate words. These words could be arranged as I saw fit to please the audience of my mind. But to communicate, I have to consider the presence, the needs of the Other . . . . Just as I begin to reflect on this, three other words, uninvited, make a sudden appearance: *Child, water, wind.* It is already clear that this can only complicate matters . . . .

3.

Where do the words come from, and where do they go? The voice of the child. There is a place in the mind, I say, and that is where the words appear and disappear. It is a place that has no name — although we call it "memory," or sometimes "dream." Something comes into us, and later out of us, in ways we cannot guess or foretell. There are times when we assemble all the words into one word: *love*. And as long as the feeling lasts, we say and are ready to believe: love is the water and the wind, in which the syllables and letters form and take shape. Love is the face that has nothing to show, nothing to tell. It is the "no-word" sounding soundlessly with the "no-voice" that the mind has learned to trust and believe in . . . .

Whether or not the child is still here, still listening, we cannot tell. But the no-voice is still present, carrying on its incessant, urgent whispering in the mind. What its voiceless urging implies, surely, is the death of words—somehow similar to the death of snow on black asphalt. This love then—of which and for which there is no utterance—offers only the nourishment of loss. For even if it could speak, it would possess the shortest, bleakest vocabulary: *hello, goodbye*.

We learn then that what is said between these two words is only of minor importance. It is even possible that one is implicit in the other; so we are really left with the single word: *goodbye*.

Goodbye to a place. Goodbye to a name. Goodbye to remember. This is the nature of one, of many, of all uncertain things. Now if only we could see the face of the child, anticipate the direction of the wind, locate a source for the clear water of the soul . . . .

1987/1989

Kafka's Bridge

1.

We cannot tell, of course, just how this happened. But we can imagine that the image must have appeared to him at a moment of great intensity. That it came with a sudden rush of feeling—one of surprising directness and clarity—although with much yet to be defined. Perhaps for a while then it was still that familiar object enclosed in its own space: that taut swaying structure he had seen many times before, both in actual form and in dream. But then, as he looked closer, there was much that puzzled him as to the true nature of its existence. It appeared then, in spite of its bulk and material force, as a more ambiguous structure: a monument to human longing, to the restless desire for passage across divided shores . . . .

Thus as the bridge augmented, magnified, he began to compare his being *here* with its being *there*. The sound of the wind, the fragrance of the sea air entered the realm where dream and memory coincide. He began to feel what it would be like to hang suspended, totally exposed to the caprice of weather. As though its "body" had become his body. And he could watch the dark-winged birds diving past, pausing at the top of the taut, swaying steel cables and towers . . . . As he plunged further into this transformed state, the wind played upon the surface of his skin, forcing him to feel its impact, to become part of its steel and wind-tuned song . . . .

2.

Let us admit now what we must admit—that the reader may well perceive this as fantasy, wondering how the present writer could allow *his* imagination to go this far. I can only say in response: How else could Kafka have written his famous story of the bridge that "awoke" one day and saw itself as imprisoned, condemned to carry the weight of human longing and restlessness?

How else could he have intuited that bizarre transformation: the tremors, the spasms, the uncoiling of that vast structure, that monument to human ingenuity and desire? Above all, how was he able, with passion and convincing detail, to bring us to that climactic moment when it began trembling with its new-found intimations of "consciousness"? Then started that fatal turn, twisting loose from its foundations, making that enormous, grinding effort *to look back upon itself*....

3.

For years now I have planned to reread the story. But each time persuaded myself to be content with the version imprinted in my memory. It was better, I thought, to leave it there. Better to consider now what happens *in real life*, where for any number of reasons, one bridge after another has come crashing down. For I recall, as we all do, how after each of these disasters a parade of experts appear, all offering rational explanations. How from then on the air is filled with their absurd, ambiguous testimony. And of course nothing is accomplished....

I suppose that we could end here, on this skeptical, despairing note. But the story of our own bridge, which only recently survived a major earthquake, sustaining only minor damage, may offer a more hopeful example. For after many years of neglect, of taking its existence for granted, we have at last been sensible enough to begin correlating its existence with our own. We have instituted a celebration of the anniversary of its completion, honoring the workers and engineers who sacrificed so much to bring it into being. And just this year—as an example of civic pride—we have garlanded its towers with hundreds of small, friendly lights. Thus we have taken steps to ensure its appeal, not only in the present, but for years to come. We can only hope that our example will be noticed, and that similar steps will be taken—before it is too late—in other parts of the country....

1988/1990

The Bridge To Dream / To Remember

1.

For years we lived with both bridges in place, satisfied that this arrangement offered an adequate choice of direction. The names alone, it seemed, served to clarify our intentions whenever we set forth on our various journeys. If asked about this, we might have replied: our need now is to cross *The Bridge To Dream*. Or with equal certainty: *The Bridge To Remember*.

Only a few of these journeys (do we need to explain?) have turned out well. In retrospect we have made the wrong choice over and over again. And with each of these mistakes, concluded that going the other way would have made more sense . . . . It is only recently that it has occurred to some of us that we need another alternative. Some of our leading citizens and lawmakers, acting from a variety of motives, are suggesting now that a third bridge must be constructed. A few speculative drawings have even appeared in the daily press; these purport to show it is entirely possible to connect this with the two already in use . . . .

2.

The *Remember/Dream Commission*, as it is popularly called, has had its first meeting. As many of us have expected, the advocates and opponents are sticking to their already announced allegiances. The arguments offered are almost impossible to follow. Instead of dealing with practical matters—the cost of such an enterprise, how it would deal with the worsening traffic situation— there is much concern with the "symbolism" of a third bridge. Much talk about an appropriate name: how could it be reconciled with the metaphoric content of *Dream* and *Remember*? No wonder our citizens are confused. For all this is creating a situation where one part of the population may well consider the two bridges already in place as separate, hostile entities: mutually exclusive and forever apart . . . .

3.

A bridge to dream. A bridge to remember. We name them separate when we need the separation. We name them together when these names appear as aspects of each other. But somewhere else—in another part of the mind—possibility beckons and necessity urges yet another (still unnamed) alternative. And still no one has suggested, as of this writing, that the structural engineer, the traffic expert sit down with the poet, the psychologist, the metaphysician and try to find out what this obsession with motion is all about. For according to the last figures, more than 25 million of our citizens move in any given year. And to accommodate the extravagant illusion that a better life can be found elsewhere, more highways, bridges are constantly being suggested . . . . If we were really to dream, really to remember, wouldn't this begin to subside? For if we began to confront what sends us forth on these endless forays and excursions, wouldn't it become plain what we have wasted and destroyed in the process?

But as things stand now, we continually retrace our departures and entrances, turning and returning across the same roadways, not willing or not able to name a single belief or allegiance to what was once—in some dream, some lost memory, the promise of arrival . . . .

1987/1990

The Awakening

for Zdena

... *Does it happen this way?* The question startles her. It comes, in a moment of reverie, after the more urgent questions have apparently been dealt with. Questions that have centered on the ending of one phase of her life and the beginning of another. She wonders if the difference now is that those others were concerned with getting ready to move, with the uncertainties of new circumstance. Facing a threshold that both beckoned and repelled.... It takes her a while to realize that what she is perceiving is not a further difficulty, but a convergence, on the plane of being, within herself .... She feels ready to accept this, even though there is no single defining image. She recalls and reaches for a photograph—taken some time ago—that she has felt was most herself. She holds it up toward the mirror .... No, she tells herself, without photograph, without mirror. She is surprised then at the sudden sound of her voice, speaking her name. At first what it summons is the child—those mysterious encounters and events—and then the woman. And through all of this, the changing outlines of form and figure. Then later the name takes its place among the nameless, the unnamed. Takes its place in a world of things, a world of people ....

*

... She understood that this was an "awakening." A departure from how she had seen herself, how others had seen her. So perhaps a different name was needed, one that would reflect this new state of being. Perhaps some name taken from nature. *Cloud. Bird. Tree. Spring.* She smiled at the extravagance of this, and just for a moment, it seemed the photograph and the mirror were smiling back .... She felt fully awake now. More awake, more alert than ever before. So this is what it's like, she thought. This is what I've become. And then, quite unexpectedly: this is what we have become. She heard herself speaking aloud again, alternating her given name with the name taken from nature. She could not be sure at this moment—and perhaps from now on—who the speaker was and what the listener might be hearing 1990

Portrait of the Man: As Novelist

... Suddenly he was famous. It was not what he intended, worked for, thought about—but there it was. He had written and published a novel; a lot of copies had been sold. He had been photographed and interviewed and invited to parties. Many parties. As he sifted through the events that led up to this, he recalled a specific morning when something—a kind of story—had appeared in his mind. It dealt with people he had seen only briefly and had not until then considered writing about. But that morning their voices, their faces entered the room. And when they remained, became more and more prominent, more *real*, he knew that these uninvited guests would not leave ....

*

... The day arrived when his phone stopped ringing. There were no more photographs, no more interviews, no more parties. The room where he worked each day seemed emptier. The days were much too long; the nights opened into a space, a time that excluded him. It was time, he thought, to write another book. He set to work devising a plot, inventing characters—all the while missing the ease, the flow of the first book. Finally he was able to put words on paper, to write pages and chapters, until it all came together .... When the book came out, there were reviews, a few photographs, even a few interviews. But there were no parties. He reread the reviews for a clue. One in particular caught his attention: the letdown experienced here was part of a "second-book syndrome."

*

... This remained in his mind in the months that followed. He wrote now from habit, from the knowledge that he had the discipline to see it through to the end. He was able then to write this third book with no great effort. And after a suitable interval, to bring a fourth book to completion. He was by then no longer surprised or disappointed that there were no more photographs, interviews, or parties . . . . He was, however, somewhat surprised when one morning the uninvited guests of his first book appeared. He offered them something to eat and to drink. They seemed indifferent, remote. He knew then that this time they would leave of their own accord—at a moment and for reasons of their own choosing . . . .

1988/1990

More About Stones

for Bob Arnold

1.

Facing the stone-covered hill, there is an echo, a reverberation, that reaches into some unfilled corner of his mind. Curious that it suggests both a presence and an absence—unconnected with this landscape or any particular memory. Perhaps it is something more inherent, innate, carried over from a time when the stones were simply there. A time when the stones were used for protection against the wind or an advancing enemy....

He walks a few steps, looks at the trees, the sky. Almost lost in the reverie, he cannot be sure that what he sees next is real or imagined. At a distance, in the uncertain light, is a group of vague, shuffling figures. As they move closer, he notices they are wearing a kind of peasant clothing, costumes that belong to another place and time.... He stands apart, watching them, as they take out and unfold crude burlap sacks and begin gathering the stones. There is no apparent difference between what they pick up and place inside the sacks and what they scrutinize and throw back upon the ground....

After a while, on a signal from one of the men, they stop and gather in a circle. They begin an animated discussion in a language he has never heard before. One after another they reach into the sacks, take out a few stones, hold them up to the light. They seem to be responding to a challenge, as though their choices must be justified to each other and to their leader....

2.

...He stands alone in a darkened room. A stone glows on the table in front of him. He picks it up, raises it to his mouth. He blows upon it, warming it with his breath. Was it a weapon or a tool? He looks for clues that might define the difference. It seems shaped beyond what was needed for any particular use. Whoever did this, he thinks, was motivated by some obscure intuition. Perhaps a notion that the extra shaping might add something—

148

something to please and surprise—each time one picked it up. He returns the stone to the surface of the table. The unknown maker—a figure he cannot summon or define—beckons to him across the centuries....

3.

The stones are fitted, set into a wall. Those who walk by the wall a thousand years later wonder at the seamless joining. How did those builders, with only the crudest tools, carry out their task? Strange that this thought comes to him one afternoon in a museum. He is looking at a collection of stones placed in haphazard fashion on the museum floor. There is a title for this "work." The card on the wall gives the name, the name of the artist, the date of completion . . . . But why are the stones *here,* and not in the earth where they belong? He enacts a scene where the artist is asked the same question. The artist hesitates, shrugs, then responds, "I've wondered about that too."

4.

A stone is a stone. It is not, in itself, a sign or signifier. Bereft of any elevated status—as monument, amulet, or emblem—it retains its "stoneness." What is our difficulty in accepting this? Is it some need to fill those unfilled corners of the mind? To perceive it as this stone—or even *our* stone? As though to place upon it the burden of the story of who and what we are.

That we may appear to be more than the sum of our appearances and disappearances. That the scale of our small lives may be decisively altered by incising upon its surface the enduring name. And if that is asking too much, perhaps just a few distinctive markings to indicate it has passed into and through our hands....

... We have come back then—have we not?—to that stone-covered hill, to those vague, shuffling figures whose reality we can neither dispose of nor verify. Come back then by some curious, circuitous route to that nameless, unmarked hill—where we always need protection against a stronger wind, an advancing, ever more ambiguous enemy....

1987/1990

Wind, Says the Voice

1.

Wind: the bone-flutes of memory. Here on a cliff overlooking the northern sea, we stare at the darkening sky, the churning water. Birds circle and descend. Water cutting into rock, a dark line wavers, widens across a strip of yellow sand.... What are we looking at, what confronts us here? The chill we feel is more than what plays upon the flesh. Something of dream, the untraceable reminder, the return of something lost. Perhaps the overthrow of yesterday.... Yesterday when, a few miles inland, we watched a placid duet of clouds and sky, the rise of unknown birds above the winding river. And on that leisurely, peaceful walk, we passed a whole series of neat, compassionate gardens....

... Here now the errant wind disturbs, altering the scale of our perceptions, bringing unwelcome reminders that make us guess and fear.... And so the scene shatters; the fragments that emerge appear on a different plane, across a world of time.... A procession of dark figures moves across the sand. (Who are they? Where have they come from?) The answer comes across a great distance, traversing a memory, an inheritance longer, deeper than our own. It tells us these are the Trojan women searching the stained, littered beaches—among the bodies broken and becalmed—for the face that only yesterday lighted their waking eyes....

Wind, says the voice. It is not their loss that concerns you. You have no friends, no relatives among the slain. No mothers, no daughters among the keening women. No friends to console you—to compose elegies (and eulogies) for the grieving—among those who so quietly, gracefully finger their guitars. We see you instead conspiring with Fire, and while we watch this churning water, you make furnaces of our trees.... Are you then, as some have said, the one who batters and erodes our monuments, the force that scatters the syllables of our broken, rootless words?

2.

Wind, have you returned to another time, another setting? I hear through the swaying branches morning being drummed out of season. Is this then your other face, which brings to an end your little lyric dance among the leaves? How is it we are still—after all these years—so full of plans and expectations? Still placing so much trust in insulated wiring, in copper pipes installed in our houses? Perhaps we should move to the plains, where the grotesque, shattered fences point toward a deadpan sky. Landscape of dead automobiles, of stained, disconnected bathtubs, of ripped, water-soaked mattresses . . . .

Wandering through those twisted spaces, a bewildered child sifts through the debris for a cat, a doll, a soft companion for his broken sleep . . . . Wind, we place all this before you, inviting inspection of spaces you have swirled through, callous, undeniable. Isn't it time and more than time to withhold this fury and vengeance? Let us be sensible, set aside our differences, and begin to negotiate some sort of treaty. On our part we agree to your right to appear and disappear without prior notice. We ask in turn that you consider our joint status in regard to all living things. So let us clarify our standing here among sheep and elephants and dancing bears . . . .

. . . Invader of caves, inspirer of eyes staring into craters, we offer you these mounds opening into air, this horn of plenty, the ghosts of these dead automobiles. Leave us the spirit and souls of those who have strayed into the nameless spaces of dry canyons—where at night they form the outlines of shapes we remember under the full moon. Help us to bring them back from their secret homes, where they have taken up residence among coyotes and timberwolves. We realize there is no use sending out searching parties, but perhaps with your help we can . . . .

1979/1990

151

The Jugglers

We live in a time of surprising, even heroic transformations. Heroic at times, but absurd at others. I still remember, for instance, when the Myshkin brothers earned their living in the most ordinary way: as handymen or doing rough carpentry. Who could have imagined that, only a few years later, they would appear onstage, billed as THE AMAZING MYSHKINS. It started, so I'm told, one afternoon when, becoming totally bored with the routine of work, they started a game of catch with their tools.

I have it on good authority that one or the other of them then began juggling his screwdrivers and pliers. Some time later they worked out some routines and began inviting a few friends to witness and even join in the fun. One of these friends, it turned out, was performing as a clown in a local nightclub. He invited them to join him onstage one evening. . . .

*

They were an immediate hit. The sight of hammers, screwdrivers, files, even small saws flying through the air entranced audiences. At some point they introduced a variation in their performance, stepping down from the stage and performing in the aisles. They also began recruiting members of the audience to stand between them (those brave or foolish enough to participate) while the tools passed back and forth. I'm also told that, later on, they refined this part of the act by limiting the choice of objects to hammers and sickles. But whether this was pure symbolism or meant to be a special challenge to their dexterity, I could never be sure. . . .

*

Success it seems is no cure for boredom. For a while yes, but given the restless spirit, that too begins to pall. I think what happened was this: they began to miss the genuine work with tools, perhaps some pride of craftsmanship. Back in their workshop,

152

one of them reached into the bin where they stored scraps of wood. He nailed together a few pieces, and saw that it formed the letter A. His brother then nailed together the letter Z. One nodded to the other; they gestured back and forth in wordless understanding. Another enterprise, profitable or not, but surely pleasurable, was under way.

*

I never had time to attend any of their performances. But those who did said it was great fun. The sight of those letters flying through the air was even more enjoyable than the screwdrivers and pliers .... The act came to an end, I understand, one evening in a crowded nightclub when they tried to get the whole alphabet in the air at the same time. Some of the letters struck some of the patrons; others crashed into the huge mirror at the back of the bar....

I heard nothing further about them for some time. Then from someone close to them—one of the few they continued to permit access to their workshop—came this news: they had resumed work on the letters. But now they were working only with choice, expensive woods. They were experimenting with different wood stains and an array of waxes—sending for materials that can only be obtained in certain tropical forests, in certain remote parts of the world....

1990

153

The Poet Digs a Hole

. . . He stands in an open field, shovel in hand, staring at the ground. He turns, raises his head, as some small dark birds descend toward a nearby tree. His attention lingers there, and beyond them toward the motion of some drifting clouds. He waits a few moments longer, then returns to his shoveling . . . . *What has brought him here?* Whatever it is, we are intrigued by his dedication to this simple, purely physical task. Watching as he bends and scoops, it occurs to us that, with this much effort, he must have more in mind than an ordinary hole. We imagine a prolonged period of meditation, reflection before making the choice of location. We even envision an earlier scene: at the hardware store, he questions the owner as to the merits of the various shovels offered for sale.

*

. . . Still no clue as to what has brought him here. We concede though that whatever a poet digs may be considered a "poetic" hole. That is, one shaped and formed in response to some complicated intention, the eventual form of which is not immediately apparent . . . . We were about to say more, but the thought is interrupted by the arrival of a group who position themselves nearby. We can hear enough of their voices to identify them as critics and theorists. This is confirmed by occasional words—*metaphoric, metonymic, opacity, transparency*—that fill the air with a strange, disembodied sound . . . .

*

. . . He continues raising and lowering the shovel with a rapid concentrated motion—but then more slowly, with frequent pauses, staring at the trees, the birds, the sky . . . . We are startled by the sudden motion as he lets the shovel fall, jumps down into the hole. He walks back and forth, testing the ground. It seems he has found the ground too soft, too damp. He climbs out, picks up the shovel, begins refilling the hole . . . .

*

... A minor disappointment or a major setback? A momentary impulse or part of some enduring passion? We cannot even begin to answer these questions. We do not even know whether this hole—poetic or ordinary—was meant to build upon, or to bury something in. And if the latter, was it to contain a treasure, or to hide a guilty secret? Whatever the case, the poet has again undertaken a project involving intense labor, leading to another absurd outcome. And not only the labor, but the purchase of a shovel—when his imagination could have invented one. One that could be lying on the ground next to *the red wheelbarrow, standing in the rain, beside the white chickens.*

... As an alternative, he might have moved closer to the watchful group of critics and theorists. Close enough to hear what they were saying and perhaps to follow their advice. He might then, however, have moved to another location—and begun the same process over again . . . . But perhaps the thought of this is too much, and we may be ready now to turn our attention elsewhere.
... Let us leave it then for some future archaeologist puzzling over a series of holes apparently started and then abandoned—with not a single artifact in sight.

1988/1990

The Cheering Section

... Yes, it is unlikely. But say it is autumn—with all its sounds, smells, colors—and we have come here in real time, in the real world. Our presence then is evidence, physical as the striped clothing on the striped field. (Not memory, not dream.) And we are not merely present in the flesh, but just here, in this row of seats among these noisy, absorbed partisans. So much a clear and conscious choice that we can offer allegiance to the locals, deny affection to the visitors .... Voices getting louder by the moment. If we add our own or withhold them, will it make any difference? But what happens to the one voice when it is absorbed, totaled into thousands, into millions?

... Breathe quickly now, breathe heavily. Watch the locals, appropriately clad in red and white, leap into the air, clasp each other in triumph. And since we have become partisans and believers—we are of them, as they are of us—why not do the same? *But what of the losers?* Of course, we do not have to think of them, not even glance in their direction. And yet, isn't this the moment when we can most afford to be generous? Still we may live better without these reminders: how they sit in the hollowed space, sprawled on the narrow benches, slumped and dejected ....

*

... Yes, I have written these words. Words that only touch the surface, presenting a world in which there are only partisans and believers. But where are the specific emotions, anything as personal, as inevitable as rage and delight? Emotions we were bound to express as children—not as opposing choices, but brought together: *the outrage of delight.* Nothing here either about the nature of the contest. How precisely it defines the separation, and the coming together, of the "not yet" and the "no longer." So that this little play of winners and losers is surrogate to our dreams of defeat, and defeat of our dreams .... But hold on —what's going on there?—that group of children on the playing field. Are they locals or visitors? Without uniforms it's impossible to tell. All we can cheer now is the season itself 1988/1990

Who Waits for Whom?

. . . A brief response to what perhaps does not need to be taken seriously. What may be considered no more than a minor provocation. Well, no need for long-winded introductions. The plain fact is that a curious document has recently come into my possession. As to the source, how it got here, I am not permitted to say. I can reveal that it is evidently a response to my essay: "Who Waits for Whom?" (*The Enigma Review*, vol. 1, no. 4, 1986). An essay in which I put forth the view that not all of us are waiting for His return, that for a good many this would be either undesirable or impossible.

. . . Now comes this document which presents evidence—some of it with that surface gloss that makes it appear convincing—that our own waiting is a minor matter, hardly measurable on the cosmic scale. The writer of this piece (using a pseudonym) argues that it is His waiting, through countless aeons, that has created a being for whom the term "infinite patience" has almost a literal meaning. So that when we ask, What is *He* waiting for? we are coming closer to the true state of things.

The question is relevant *because* it is unanswerable—for its suggestion that it is not for us but for Him to answer. That answer, when it comes, will be an *event* originating and contained within the bounds of His boundless mind. And therefore not available to our own limited understanding. What we can, however, reasonably assume is that the nature of His being is what He both is and is going to be. So that all the arguments over His reported "death" are both exaggerated and premature. We have only to put aside the story of Genesis—as it has been read and commented upon—and convert it to its true meaning. For according to this view, Genesis was nothing more than an alteration of circumstance, a clue to the emergence of a Guiding Force. All that He has been—it is at last clear—is almost nothing compared to what *He has yet to be*. With that recognition—when it finally occurs—we may then at last set foot upon a stage whereon is performed a grander, as-yet-undreamed-of destiny   1990

The Universal Delivery Service

1.

The question of how things get from here to there—which is taken so much for granted—has puzzled me for years. It may be my natural pessimism, but it still surprises me that a letter arrives where intended. The same with packages, parcels, foodstuffs, artworks, furniture, etc. This in a world where, as seasoned observers agree, chaos and even apocalypse are never far away. Still I admit a kind of order—at least on this level—does persist. My view of all this, in any case, is soon bound to be altered, as I have recently been offered a position within the Service. I have accepted this, as a kind of experiment, with the understanding that I may leave at any time....

2.

...I am pleased of course to have an office of my own. But on entering, I see there is not much reason for rejoicing. For one thing, the room is small, the furniture nondescript, the windows smudged. Also, it is located in an unused part of the building, which seems to be an old warehouse. The only signs of activity are the unmarked trucks that, about once an hour, appear at the loading dock. Men in dark uniforms load and unload boxes; this is done quickly, almost mechanically, with gestures instead of speech. As far as I can see through the filthy glass, the boxes are of a uniform size and shape, with no apparent difference between those delivered and those taken away....

3.

I have been here over a week. The telephone was installed several days ago, but so far there have been no calls. I have kept busy arranging and rearranging an assortment of catalogues of various kinds of equipment and machinery. Aside from the trucks, the only contact with the outside world is the mail. Each day, as I open the door, I find a dozen or more envelopes littering the floor. These invariably have printed messages on the cover:

Please fill out and return. Last chance. Opportunity of a lifetime. I have delayed opening any of these, since none are addressed to me, until I receive further instructions. . . .

4.

This morning an unsigned note arrived. (At last, something with my name on the envelope!) The brief typed message is that all mail received so far—and until further notice—is to be marked *Please forward as instructed.* There is no indication, however, as to where any of this is to be sent. I can only assume that, sooner or later, the information will arrive . . . . A few days later a second envelope arrives. I open it and read the brief message: *Please disregard previous notice. Material in your office is now subject to revised procedure. In a few days, everything will be picked up and turned over to the Central Office. You will then be assigned to different duties . . . .*

5.

. . . Sitting here in the empty office, ready to gather my few belongings and leave. Everything else left with the truck an hour ago. I tried to engage the driver in conversation, but his replies were brief and noncommittal. One thing, though, caught my attention: when I mentioned that I was awaiting reassignment, he responded, "The U.D.S. goes anywhere and everywhere." I suddenly realized that this included me as well. I told him this would be difficult for me, as I had obligations here. He shrugged and said, "As far as the U.D.S. is concerned, space is no barrier, time is no obstacle."

6.

. . . I see now that I will have to resign. I realize this means I can no longer observe the workings of "the system" from the inside. Still I have learned much in a short time, even though in a larger sense my experiment must be considered a failure. Perhaps if I could have entered at a level more consonant with my abilities, more could have been accomplished and learned. I might have had more opportunity for contact with the shadowy figures who design policies and procedures . . . . As it is, the question remains: Is there indeed a delivery system that can go "anywhere and everywhere"? Deep inside me I find this, curiously, both reassuring and frightening. I suppose this reaction may be due to the belief—instilled at an early age—that borders and boundaries are not only necessary but may at times even be considered as sacred . . . .

1987/1990

The Fourth Step

So much has been written about the first three that my reference to a "fourth step" may not be taken seriously. While prepared for the rejection, I offer this as a possibility. But first, let me honor the courage and perseverance of those who have "stayed the course", and have accepted their new state of being. What seems to have happened is that even the most strongly convinced have acknowledged the stirrings of a new wave of confusion and discontent. We have the testimony of those who gave evidence as to the validity of their transformation, but now admit the continuing erosion of their created self.

One of them, I recall, made quite a point of this at a gathering which I happened to attend. He said in a loud voice and with a sweeping gesture that included all around him: "But of course we have all invented ourselves." The problem now, he went on, was to find the way back to who we were *originally*, at the beginning of our lives. It was in that split between the original and the created self that we now experienced a kind of fragmentation. "Taking those three steps," he said, "was a wonderful, challenging experience. The trouble was it was just not enough—not enough to last."

*

It was this encounter, and later a number of others, that led me to the notion of a fourth step. For those unacquainted with the theory, the ritual that led to "The Three Steps to Self-Awareness," I will summarize them briefly: Step One is *ordeal*; Step Two is *pilgrimage*; Step Three is *transformation*. At this point I want to be careful not to overstate the case. There must have been quite a large number for whom this was enough. They had embarked upon a journey into their own interiors. And they had discovered capacities and qualities beyond expectation and dream. For a while then, as I've already indicated, they could experience the satisfied passion of the completed journey.

*

I hope I have not relied too heavily on a too familiar metaphor. But I find the reference to "journey" to be the simplest, most useful expression here. So once more, there was the realization—sooner and more intensely among those with a greater sensibility—that with all their journeying, they had not arrived at "the place." I will add now that it is time to change *they* to *we*. For we too have come to a place we have been permitted to glimpse but not to enter. Have come to a door that might open with a spoken word. But the word does not come to our lips. . . .

*

. . . For the longest time, we could only stand there staring, waiting. And then somehow we felt a curious sensation that words were already inscribed on that door which we had to decipher. We could not be sure, but it was as if, after a while, letters appeared and formed these words: *For Saints and Martyrs Only*. Considering who and what we are, perhaps the word can now be named: *redemption*. The word that contains and modifies all those other words. The word that is still whispered, pronounced only in private. How much longer, we wonder, will this continue? Perhaps until we are aware of and prepared to take THE FOURTH STEP. It seems obvious now that this must indeed be the case. And yet when we think of how difficult it has been to have come this far, think of how many of the brightest and the best have fallen along the way. . . .

1988/1990

Next Is This

... So much talk about "the word." What it is, what it ought to be, how it should be used, etc. And of course this includes the "right" word in the right place, the right time. But when a word suggests itself—comes forward and asks to be recognized—how can I prove it meets these requirements? I can only say that it is *here* and insists on being named. As in the present moment I reply to this insistence and type the letters: *n-e-x-t*. Staring at this I'm suddenly reminded of a line I once wrote: "We are left then with a choice between silence and nonsense." I seem prepared to take the risk and make the choice. For it occurs to me that the sense of it may be present to all kinds of people in all kinds of situations. It may be a poet who thinks of it, or a scientist, a barber, a fruit vendor. And if this is a desired moment, we may say to ourselves, *at last, at last.* And if we are facing what we have feared, sought to avoid, then we may wait and urgently hope someone else will step forward.

*

... So it is when we feel stymied, suspended between an intractable "not yet" and, after a barely noticeable interval, the dismal announcement of a "no longer." What then have we missed? What failure of attention has caused us to turn away at just that moment which was to be completely ours? I refer to the arrival of just that "next" which was to be genuinely *new*—rather than more of the same. It is just then, I suppose, that we fall back upon the trite images spawned by tiresome references to faith and luck. This in spite of our long experience that there can be no anticipation without apprehension. And it is at this very moment that "the unprecedented" comes into view ....

*

We may be brought then to consider what happens in nature. As the poet/naturalist reminds us, there may yet appear *forms that break step with knowing.* A fish that flies, a bird that swims. Whatever exotic beings are still coming ashore, their shapes and colors as yet undetermined, unimagined. But even within this pres-

ent time, studying the motion of a single wave, we have some-
thing to learn. We can watch it being formed, rising, poised at its
apex, then released for its sudden descent.... What this one wave
engenders—with the sun, the light, the wind as variables—can
be as new as *never before*, as ancient as *always was*....

*

This ends for now my reflection on the word *next*. Before putting
these words on paper, I assure you, I had no idea how they would
come out. It is only now that it occurs to me: *rhymes with text*. As if to
say: whatever appears here has its own reason for being. If we can
accept this, we can look beyond the familiar, beyond the need
for context. I like to think that we can venture this far, in this sim-
ple way, beyond restricted space. And having established a
sense of confidence that we can survive even without an "event
horizon," why not be prepared to welcome the *as yet unrealized?*

1987/1990

Afterword

Once we leave behind the residues of either / or, and for or against, we enter a different, more pluralistic realm. This may be apparent with no more than a closer look at the book's title. Words like *truth* and *war* may suggests a whole range of meanings even within the mind of a single reader. As for *dream-game,* where there are no fully realized associations, a greater effort may be called for. Significant clues are part of the dream-game, but its rules and procedures, its invisible, unsettling influence, may be even more difficult to trace.

The first grouping is of those pieces which deal with the theme of what we have come to call "Spirituality"—not confined to any one religion, nor to religion itself.

from *Tracking Stations*
   "Destruction of the Temple"
   "The Refugees / The Pilgrims"
   "The Leopards / The Temple"
   "Reading the Text"
   "The Message / The Messenger"
   "The Choice"
   "The Loaves / The Fishes"
   "The Dark Pattern"
   "The Return of Sadhu"
   "The Choice"

On Politics, War, and the Effects of War:

from *Tracking Stations*
   "Flight Patterns"
   "The Departure / The Return"
   "The Refugees / The Pilgrims"
   "The Situation Room"
   "The Retreat of the Leaders"
   "The Given Day"
   "The Trial of Two Cities"

On the City as Concept and Metaphor:

from *Tracking Stations*
  "Leaving the City"
  "The Given Day"
  "The Shrinking City"
  "The News from Dronesville"
  "The Trial of Two Cities"

All this is offered to focus, but not to limit, the reader's own exploration. In addition to the cross-referencing already indicated by these groupings, there can be a briefer alternative: that of pairing. That is, between two pieces that especially reflect upon each other. Examples of this: "The Cage: The Performance" along with "The Actor: Farewell & Return." "A Stone Taking Notes" and "More About Stones." "Say We Are Going" and "No Time for Gestures." "The Door to Have" and either "The Knock" or "The Trouble with Keys." "The Contest" and "The Photographers." A special case is the linking of "The Door to Have" with "Question of a Shovel"—the only two pieces in the book that end with a poem.

Lawrence Fixel, March 1991